Last years of steam
Paddington~
Wolverhampton

BR Standard Class 5 No 73128 restarts after taking water at Princes Risborough with a Warsop-Wembley Hill football special. This was run in connection with the England versus West Germany Schoolboy International at Wembley on 25 April 1964. Brian Stephenson

The evening sun highlights 2-6-2T
No 4176 leaving Hatton with the 18.05
Birmingham-Leamington on 3 July
1984.   *Paul Riley*

Last years of steam

Paddington~ Wolverhampton

Laurence Waters

BLP

Author's Note
Although titled The Last Years of
Steam: Paddington-Wolverhampton, *I
have for completeness included within
the text the early history of both the
line and its services. Also included is
the North Warwicks route as its traffic
formed an integral part of the
workings in the Birmingham area.
The photographic content, however,
with just a few exceptions has been
limited to within the period 1953-
1965.*

Publisher's Note
This book was first published in 1988 and
statements made then were current. Many of
these may well have been overtaken by
subsequent events.

First published 1988 by Ian Allan Ltd
This impression 1997

ISBN 1 901945 05 7

Published by Book Law Publications and printed
by Ian Allan Printing Ltd at its works at
Coombelands in Runnymede, England.

Contents

Front cover:
**On 29 August 1962 the 6.30am
Birkenhead-Paddington is seen here
between Olton and Solihull with 'King'
class 4-6-0 No 6021 *King Edward II* in
charge.** M. Mensing

Rear cover:
**'Large Prairie' No 4120 leaves Acocks
Green & South Yardley with the
12.50pm Birmingham Snow Hill-
Leamington Spa service on 13 February
1962.** M. Mensing

Right:
**Steam hard at work, as No 4925
Eynsham Hall climbs to Fosse Road
summit, south of Leamington Spa on
29 April 1957.** R. H. Short

Far right:
**'Castle' class 4-6-0 No 7022 *Hereford
Castle* is seen on Hatton Bank with the
08.45 Margate-Wolverhampton on
20 June 1964.** Gerald T. Robinson

Preface

By the turn of the century, the railway mania that had gripped this country for so long was rapidly coming to an end. With most of the major lines completed there seemed little more left to do. At this time, however, the Great Western Railway was known, with some disrespect, as the 'great way round'. This was certainly an apt name for some of its routes, and in the ensuing years the company undertook a series of improvements in an attempt both to speed up services and to lose this unfortunate image. New cut-off routes were completed at Badminton during 1903, at Castle Cary in 1906 and lastly the Bicester cut-off in 1910. This final link at last removed the stigma of the 'great way round' tag.

The Great Western was obviously pleased with its new shorter routes, for it promoted them with some enthusiasm; particularly the route to Birmingham, as it meant they could at last compete with the LNWR for the lucrative Birmingham and Wolverhampton traffic. For many years the *Holiday Haunts Guide* extolled both the pleasure of living and travelling along the route as the following extracts convey.

'The route between Paddington and Birmingham by way of Bicester is rapidly populating many delightful places both as travel and residential centres. The line from Denham to High Wycombe serves a district of unrivalled beauty. At Gerrards Cross, the air is exceptionally pure and particularly beneficial to people with lung troubles.'

This then is how the last main line to be built in this country was promoted. It lasted for only 57 years as a main through route, a short life in railway terms.

I hope that the following pages in this book will bring back to the reader memories of the final years of steam traction over the Great Western Railway's final link.

Introduction

The direct route, as it was called, from Paddington to Wolverhampton, evolved in a way that was unusual in the building of main lines, not being planned from the start as a main through route, but gradually evolving from a series of improvements and additions to existing lines. To tell the story of the route one has to go back to 1852 when the GWR, under the guise of the Oxford & Rugby Railway Co, had extended its line from Millstream Junction, Oxford, northwards to Birmingham. Oxford had been reached as early as 1844 by the Oxford Railway Co. This company, under the guise of the GWR, reached Oxford in June of that year by way of a line from Didcot Junction. The Oxford & Rugby Railway Co had been formed in 1844, to construct a line from Oxford northwards to Fenny Compton and Rugby. Various financial problems saw the start on the new line delayed, and by the time it was completed as far as Banbury, during 1850, control of the Oxford & Rugby had passed into the hands of the GWR.

A second company, the Birmingham & Oxford Junction Railway, had been formed in 1846 to construct a line from Fenny Compton to Birmingham, a distance of some 42¾ miles. It would connect with the Oxford & Rugby Railway's route northwards at Fenny Compton. Within the Act promoting

the railway, a clause was inserted that allowed the Birmingham & Oxford Junction to lease the line to the GWR, providing ⅘th of the shareholders agreed. The LNWR strenuously opposed the building of the line, seeing it as a direct competitor with its own London-Birmingham route, which of course it was. The LNWR acted quickly, and started to buy up Birmingham & Oxford shares in an attempt to stop control of the company passing into the hands of the GWR. After a long drawn-out battle, the court deemed the action to be illegal and ruled in favour of the Birmingham & Oxford. With the problems resolved, the GWR dropped the proposed section from Fenny Compton to Rugby and instead concentrated its resources on the Birmingham & Oxford route, via Leamington. Built as a mixed gauge line throughout, it was opened for passenger traffic between Oxford and Birmingham on 1 October 1852.

The Oxford, Worcester & Wolverhampton Railway had completed its own route to Wolverhampton in April 1854, so it was quite possible at this time to reach Wolverhampton from Paddington, albeit by a long and circuitous route, that also necessitated a change of gauges at Oxford. At this time GWR services to Oxford were still operated on the broad gauge whereas

the OW&WR services from Oxford were standard. In November 1854 after many delays and much wrangling, the GWR finally reached Wolverhampton, via Birmingham and Priestfield Junction.

The Birmingham, Wolverhampton & Dudley Railway was formed to construct a mixed gauge line from Snow Hill northwards to Wolverhampton. Agreement had been reached to connect this line to the OW&WR route at Priestfield, approximately 1½ miles south of Wolverhampton. Work was started on this section during 1851. A year later, in 1852, the GWR was authorised to construct a short section, approximately ¾-mile in length, which would connect the incoming Shrewsbury & Birmingham line to the OW&WR line at Stafford Road, ½-mile north of Wolverhampton station. By August

Below:

'Modified Hall' No 7912 *Little Linford Hall* is seen here leaving Birmingham Moor Street on Sunday 26 April 1959 with an excursion to Paddington. Birmingham Moor Street was normally closed on Sundays at this time, but urgent repairs to the bridge over the London Midland lines at the south end of Snow Hill Tunnel necessitated the diversion of a few morning services on 26 April and 3 May into Moor Street.
M. Mensing

Left:
Acocks Green on 15 October 1956 with '5101' class 2-6-2T No 4112 heading the 2.0pm Leamington-Birmingham Moor Street passing Collett '2251' class 0-6-0 No 2279 (84E) on a down freight.
M. Mensing

Below left:
2-6-2T No 8100 leaves Harbury Tunnel with a Leamington-Banbury pick-up goods on 10 April 1954. T. E. Williams

Bottom:
A fine array of signals can be seen here, as No 6014 *King Henry VII* roars through Fenny Compton with the 4.10pm Paddington-Wolverhampton service, passing on its way 0-6-2T No 6671 on a limestone train from Ardley to Greaves sidings. Spring 1961.
W. Turner

1854 both lines were ready for opening, but failure of a 63ft steel girder bridge across the Winson turnpike road between Soho and Handsworth, saw the opening delayed. Once repairs had taken place and the route was satisfactorily inspected it was duly opened to passenger traffic on 14 November 1854. Wolverhampton could now be reached directly from Paddington, a distance via Oxford and Birmingham of some 142 miles.

The line was mixed gauge throughout, with standard gauge services running from Chester and Shrewsbury through to Snow Hill. Local services between Wolverhampton and Snow Hill were operated by broad gauge trains up until October 1868 when all passenger services between Wolverhampton and Snow Hill were switched to standard gauge operation. The station at Wolverhampton was interesting in that it was jointly operated for a number of years by three different railway companies;

Above:
The stationmaster at Wolverhampton Low Level discusses a point with the driver of 'Castle' No 7001 *Sir James Milne*, as he awaits the right away with the up 'Pines Express' on 7 May 1963. Note the glasses hanging around the driver's neck (French style).
Ian Allan Library

Right:
A down pick-up freight trundles into Wolverhampton Low Level on 31 August 1952.   Brian Morrison

from the south by the Oxford, Worcester & Wolverhampton Railway Co together with the Great Western, and from the north by the Shrewsbury & Birmingham Railway. Although not without its troubles and disagreements, the Oxford-Wolverhampton section had been completed within the space of just four years. Not so the southern section, via High Wycombe, as this part of the new route gradually evolved over many years and was not finally completed until 1910.

The first embryo appeared on 1 August 1854, with the opening by the Wycombe Railway Co of a 9¾-mile broad gauge branch. This ran from the GW main line at Maidenhead via Bourne End to High Wycombe. By 1 August 1862 the line had been extended to Princes Risborough and Thame. In October 1863, Princes Risborough became a junction station with the opening, again by the Wycombe Railway Co, of a 7½-mile branch from here to Aylesbury. A year later the line was extended from Thame to Kennington Junction. Worked from the start by the GWR, the Wycombe Railway was converted to standard gauge during 1870. Quite a few years were to pass before the final links on the route were forged.

When the Great Central Railway opened its main line into Marylebone during March 1899, it shared tracks south of Quainton Road with the Metropolitan Railway Co. This state of affairs had arisen because Sir Edward Watkin at the time of the proposal for this railway was the Chairman of both the Great Central and the Metro-

politan Railway companies. His great dream was to build a railway through the centre of England to the coast, and eventually via a channel tunnel to Paris. However this was not to be, as he retired in 1894, the same year that work was started on the Great Central's extension to London. Watkin's idea of connecting this line to the newly constructed Metropolitan Railway at Quainton Road and running the 40 miles into London jointly may at first have seemed a good idea, but once Watkin had retired, the two companies were soon arguing with each other about the Great Central's running rights over the Metropolitan section. This came to a head on the evening of 30 July 1898, when the new Chairman of the Metropolitan

Railway, John Bell, was instrumental in actually stopping a coal train from running on to Metropolitan metals at Quainton Road. This obviously could not go on, and the net result was the decision by the Great Central to seek an alternative route into London.

The Great Western, meanwhile, had been looking at ways of providing a shorter route to Birmingham. One such proposal put forward in 1897 was for a new line from Acton to High Wycombe. Here the old Wycombe Railway route would be upgraded to

form a new main line running through Princes Risborough to Thame and Oxford. The Great Central viewed this proposal with interest. If it could link its own route with this new line somewhere north of Quainton Road, and build a new link at the south end to Marylebone, then its running problems would be solved. Very soon the two companies were having collaborative talks, which resulted in the formation in 1899 of the Great Central Joint Committee to build and administer the new line. The

proposal finally agreed was for a new joint line, built to main line standards, running from Grendon Underwood to Northolt. At Northolt, a junction would be built and new lines would be constructed to give access to both the Great Central main line at Neasden and the GW main line at Old Oak Common.

Construction was started on the seven-mile GW section between Old Oak Common and Northolt early in 1901. Progress was such that the first part of the line, as far as Park Royal, was opened on 15 June 1903, and by 1 October 1904 it had been extended as far as Greenford. Continued good progress meant that the line was ready for opening to passengers, right through to Grendon Underwood, on 2 April 1906. The Great Central had completed its own connection from Neasden to Northolt just one month

Top:

The 1.00pm West London sidings-Shrewsbury parcels train accelerates past Old Oak Common on 19 October 1957, hauled by 'Castle' 4-6-0 No 5083 *Bath Abbey.* **The line and bridge behind the train are used for empty stock workings to and from Old Oak carriage sidings.** R. C. Riley

Left:

The joint ownership of the section between Northolt and Ashendon is clearly recorded on this trespass notice photographed near South Ruislip.
C. R. L. Coles

9

earlier on 1 March. Ironically, by the time the joint line was opened, the Great Central had patched up its differences with the Metropolitan Railway, which resulted in the formation of the Metropolitan & Great Central Joint Committee, to administer the running of the Metropolitan lines south of Quainton.

It must be remembered that the original GW proposal was to upgrade the old Wycombe Railway route from Princes Risborough to Kennington into a new cut-off route. However, by the time work was started in 1905 this proposal had been abandoned in favour of a more direct route via Bicester. The new cut-off route left the GW/GC joint line via a junction at Ashendon and ran across the Vale of Aylesbury through Bicester to connect with the main Oxford-Birmingham line at Aynho Junction, a distance of some 18¼ miles. Opened on 1 July 1910 it now gave the GWR a new shorter route from Paddington to Birmingham, reducing the distance to just 110 miles, a saving of 19 miles on the old Oxford route. It was the last main line to be constructed in this country. It was built throughout to the finest standards of the Great Western Railway, with superb brick-built stations, viaducts and bridges. At Ashendon and Aynho, flying junctions were constructed. It was a superbly engineered line and now allowed the GW for the first time to compete with the LNWR in both time and distance on the lucrative London-Birmingham and Wolverhampton services.

Routes to Stratford-upon-Avon

Stratford-upon-Avon, birthplace of William Shakespeare, is certainly one of the major tourist attractions in this country. Even before the arrival of the railway, Stratford was a popular destination, being served on a daily basis by numerous stagecoach services. The arrival of the GWR did much to promote the popular tourist image of Stratford over the ensuing years. However, it was not the first railway into the town. That honour fell to the Stratford & Moreton Tramway Co, who constructed a 4ft gauge horse-drawn tramway some 17 miles in length, between Stratford and Moreton-in-Marsh. Opened on 5 September 1826, it was extended from Moreton to Shipton-upon-Stour, eventually opening during February 1836. Essentially a goods-only line, it was licensed to carry a limited number of passengers. The whole line was taken over by the Oxford, Worcester & Wolverhampton Railway during 1847, and was converted to standard gauge in 1853. During 1887 the nine-mile section between Moreton-in-Marsh and Shipton-upon-Stour was upgraded by the GWR to allow the working of locomotive-hauled passenger trains. The original section between Moreton-in-Marsh and Stratford remained open as a goods-only tramway, still horse drawn, right up until its eventual closure in 1904.

The Great Western had reached Stratford-upon-Avon by way of a 9¼-mile mixed gauge branch which left

the main Oxford-Birmingham route at Hatton. Built by the Stratford-upon-Avon Railway Co, it was opened for passenger traffic on 10 October 1860, worked from the start by the GWR; amalgamation of the two companies did not finally take place until 1883. Three intermediate stations were provided on the branch, at Claverdon, Bearley and Wilmcote. Doubling of that section did not take place until 1939. Stratford-upon-Avon had been reached a year earlier from the south by a line from Honeybourne. Constructed by the Oxford, Worcester & Wolverhampton Railway it was opened on 12 July 1859. Thus Stratford was served by two different companies each running into its own terminus station. This situation did

Below:
A bird's-eye view of Stratford-upon-Avon, with 0-6-0 No 2211 leaving on the 8.43am to Leamington in June 1964.
T. E. Williams

Right:
No 2883 (86E) passes through Stratford-upon-Avon station with a freight for Severn Tunnel Junction on 16 August 1954. Brian Morrison

Below right:
A down empty stock train from Birmingham Moor Street passes through Yardley Wood on 8 August 1959 hauled by Mogul No 5306.
M. Mensing

not last for long, however, for a proposal to connect the two lines was duly completed with the opening on 24 July 1861 of a new 32-chain connection between the two. From this date most traffic used the OW&WR station at Stratford; the Stratford-upon-Avon Railway Co's own station at Birmingham Road became little used, eventually closing to regular passenger traffic on 1 January 1863. The new connection now allowed through running between Leamington and Worcester. Through services from Birmingham to Stratford-upon-Avon became possible by the opening of a new junction at Hatton North on 1 July 1897.

Once these lines had been opened it was not long before the nearby town of Henley-in-Arden sought to be connected to the railway. The first proposal for a railway to Henley-in-Arden was made as early as June 1861 by the Henley-in-Arden Railway Co; this was for a mixed gauge line just over three miles in length that would connect Henley-in-Arden to the nearby Great Western main line at Rowington. Although a start was made, funds soon ran out and the project was abandoned. Various other proposals were made over the ensuing years, and after many false starts a new company, the Birmingham & Henley-in-Arden Railway Co supported by the GWR, opened the line for passengers on 6 June 1894. Thus, after 33 years of waiting, Henley-in-Arden at last had its railway. This small branch was to be short-lived however, for with the opening of the North Warwicks route in 1908, Henley-in-Arden was provided with a new station on this line. For a while trains from Lapworth used this new station, but the branch gradually became redundant and was closed to passengers on 1 January 1915 and completely some two years later.

In order to open up the areas southwest of Birmingham to the potential of rail travel, the Birmingham, North Warwickshire & Stratford-upon-Avon Railway Co had been formed in 1894. Authorisation for a route from Stratford to Birmingham was obtained on 25 August of that year, but with financial support not forthcoming the scheme was temporarily abandoned. It was resurrected in July 1900 with the GWR taking over the company together with the Act to build the line. Instead of an independent route into Birmingham proposed by the original company, the GWR decided that the new line would connect with the existing route at Tyseley.

Work was started on 5 September 1905, and proceeded steadily, the line being ready to open for passenger services on 1 July 1908. The new route, known as the 'North Warwickshire line', was provided with no fewer than 10 intermediate stations on the section between Tyseley and Henley-in-Arden. It connected with the existing Hatton-Stratford line by way of a new junction at Bearley. The opening of the line also provided the GWR with a useful through route from the Midlands to the South via Cheltenham. This had been made possible by the completion during 1906 of the section of line between Honeybourne and Cheltenham. On 1 July 1908 the GWR duly inaugurated a new through service from Wolverhampton to South Wales and the southwest. A new terminus station was constructed to the south of Snow Hill at Moor Street opening to passengers on 1 July 1909. Motive power for the line was provided by two new locomotive depots, Tyseley at the north end and Leamington to the south. A small engine shed was also situated at Stratford-upon-Avon. This provided banking engines for the heavily graded section from Stratford to Wilmcote.

1
Through the Window

A Journey From Paddington to Wolverhampton on the 'Inter-City' Express in 1960

Our journey starts at Paddington, Brunel's 'Cathedral in a cutting'. Had things gone to plan, however, we might well have been leaving Euston, for that was where the GWR originally proposed that the line would terminate. That idea was dropped in 1834, when the GWR decided to build its own terminus at Paddington, so that when the line was opened as far as Taplow in June 1838, it ran to a temporary station at Bishops Road (Paddington). The GWR was rather ingenious in that it located the entrance and offices under the brick arches of the Bishops Road Viaduct. A

small engine shed and carriage sidings were located in the yard nearby.

Eventually it became apparent that this station was inadequate and in February 1853 the present-day Paddington station was proposed. Construction work was started almost immediately and on 16 January 1854 the new station was ready for use. Situated to the east of the old Bishops Road station, the main feature of the new Paddington was the vast overall roof. This consisted of three curved aisles which measured 700ft × 238ft, rising to a height of nearly 55ft above rail level. The whole station complex

covered an area of some eight acres and cost £650,000 to construct, a vast sum in those days. In 1854 the Great Western Hotel was opened in Praed Street; it was the earliest of London's railway hotels. Designed by Hardwick in the style of Louis XIV, it formed a fine frontage to the new station.

The main office accommodation, together with waiting rooms, toilets, etc, were situated on platform 1. The frequent use of the station by royalty saw the GWR install a Royal suite, which today can be identified by both the Royal and Great Western coats of arms on the entrance doors. A gradual

Left:
The attention of a pair of young train spotters is aroused as No 6006 *King George I* blasts its way out of Paddington with the 4.10pm service to Birkenhead c1958. B. Higgins

Above:
Empty stock for the service to Shrewsbury is hauled through Royal Oak station by 2-6-2T No 6135 on 3 August 1958. Brian Morrison

expansion of the station took place over the years; the removal of the broad gauge in 1892 allowed room for an additional platform. Between 1909 and 1916 a further three platforms were added, giving Paddington a total of 12 platforms for both main line and suburban use. A new aisle was added to the train shed roof during 1916, to cover the additional platforms. Built to the same design as the original, it increased the roof area at Paddington to an incredible 3½ acres. In the early 1930s more expansion work took place with the building of a new parcels depot at Bishops Road and the lengthening of platforms 2-11. The Metropolitan and Bakerloo platforms at Bishops Road were rebuilt, the name Bishops Road was dropped, and the rebuilt station became part of Paddington with platforms renumbered 13-16. These were now not only served by the LT underground trains but by GW suburban services to and from the Thames Valley.

The Metropolitan was the first of London's underground railways, opening between Bishops Road and Hammersmith in 1865; at this time it

crossed the GW main line on the level at Royal Oak. However, in 1878 a tunnel was constructed which allowed the Metropolitan trains to pass under the GW lines. The Bakerloo line had opened to Paddington on 1 December 1913.

Paddington station remained relatively unchanged although bomb damage during World War 2 necessitated repairs to both platforms and roof structures. The station celebrated its centenary in 1954, and to mark this event a commemoration plate was unveiled on platform 1. The whole of the complex at Paddington was controlled by three all-electric signalboxes: Paddington Arrival with 143 levers, Paddington Departure with 76 and Westbourne Bridge with 67.

It is now time to join the 'Inter-City Express' for the journey to Wolverhampton. As we settle in our seats, the clock on platform 1 soon moves round to 9.00am. A quick whistle from the guard and our 'King' class locomotive effortlessly moves the 11-coach train out of Brunel's great terminus; our 123-mile journey to the heart of the industrial Midlands has begun. As we slowly move under the Bishops Road Bridge we pass the large expanse of Paddington goods station, which stands on the site of the old Bishops Road terminus. Opposite on our left is the parcels depot, its platform being some 1,500ft in length. We are followed on our right as far as Royal Oak by London Transport underground trains; here they burrow under our route via Subway Junction before emerging once again at Westbourne Park.

Just to the south of Royal Oak station stands the small engine yard at Ranelagh Bridge. It was built in 1907 to allow engines arriving at Paddington to be turned and watered without having to travel back to the new shed at Old Oak Common. The yard is provided with a 65ft turntable and a 22,500gal water tank. Surprisingly there are no coaling facilities here. This small yard is rather inconveniently situated alongside many terraced houses. Standing between the yard and the large girder overbridge of the Porchester Road is the Western Region Historic Records Office, which houses many of the original GWR deeds and plans from the earliest days of the railway.

At Westbourne Park we pass the site of the old Great Western engine sheds. Built in 1852, they were demolished when the new shed at Old Oak Common was opened during 1906. On our left the Metropolitan underground trains emerge once again running for a short while on the level, before diverging away to Hammersmith. Between here and Old Oak Common the land starts to open out from the heavily built-up area we have just passed through. Across the open space on our left stands Her Majesty's prison at Wormwood Scrubs. Running behind Kensal Green gasworks on our right is the Paddington section of the Grand Union Canal. This was incorporated in 1929 by the amalgamation of the Grand Junction, the Warwick & Napton and the Warwick & Birmingham Canals; and follows the general direction of our line all the way into Warwickshire.

About three miles from Paddington we pass on our right the large locomotive and carriage servicing complex at Old Oak Common. The engine shed here is the largest on the Western Region, having an allocation approaching 180 locomotives. Unfortunately, most of the engine shed and yard is obscured by the equally large carriage sidings and sheds, the largest of which is almost 1,000ft in length.

Just beyond this large complex we leave the Bristol and South Wales main line and start our journey northwards on the new route via Old Oak Common West Junction. Passing under the North London line we are joined by the London Transport Central Line, which converges from the left. We will now run parallel with this line all the way to West Ruislip, passing a number of London Transport stations en route, many of which replaced the earlier GW halts that were originally situated on this section of track. Once past the LT station at North Acton, the large Guinness Brewery at Park Royal comes into view. The sidings on the right here provide rail access to this large complex. Between here and Hanger Lane we pass under the Uxbridge branch of the Piccadilly Line. Just to the north of Hanger Lane station we cross the River Brent, via a fine brick-built viaduct, and between Perivale and Greenford stations our

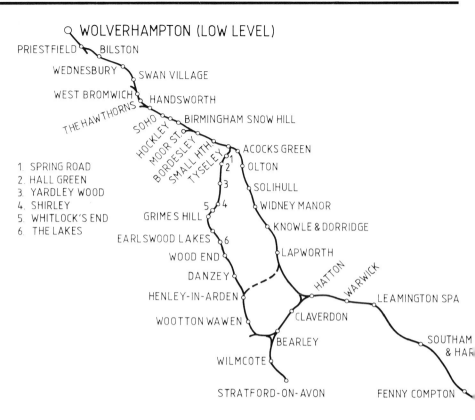

WOLVERHAMPTON (LOW LEVEL)

PRIESTFIELD — BILSTON
WEDNESBURY — SWAN VILLAGE
WEST BROMWICH — HANDSWORTH
THE HAWTHORNS — SOHO — BIRMINGHAM SNOW HILL
HOCKLEY
MOOR ST.
BORDESLEY
SMALL HTH.
TYSELEY — ACOCKS GREEN
— OLTON
— SOLIHULL
— WIDNEY MANOR
GRIMES HILL — KNOWLE & DORRIDGE
EARLSWOOD LAKES — LAPWORTH
WOOD END
DANZEY — HATTON — WARWICK
HENLEY-IN-ARDEN — LEAMINGTON SPA
WOOTTON WAWEN — CLAVERDON
BEARLEY — SOUTHAM & HAR
WILMCOTE
STRATFORD-ON-AVON — FENNY COMPTON

1. SPRING ROAD
2. HALL GREEN
3. YARDLEY WOOD
4. SHIRLEY
5. WHITLOCK'S END
6. THE LAKES

Below:
A fine portrait of No 6011 *King James I* at Old Oak Common on 5 May 1956. Evidence of a recent trip to Birmingham can be seen from the chalk inscription on the smokebox door which reads BRUM 0 MANU 5.
Brian Morrison

CROPRE

BANBU

Above:
No 5022 *Wigmore Castle* is seen here approaching Old Oak Common West Junction with the 6.45am service from Wolverhampton to Paddington, on 4 May 1957. The Central Line station at North Acton can just be seen under the bridge to the left. R. C. Riley

Right:
The 2.10pm Paddington-Wolverhampton is seen passing Park Royal on 4 August 1960. Train engine No 6017 *King Edward IV* is carrying an incorrect headcode, which should read M20. M. Pope

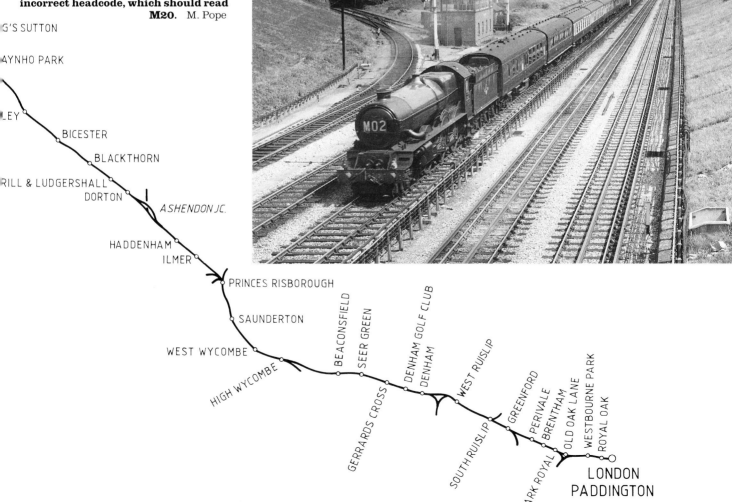

G'S SUTTON

AYNHO PARK

LEY

BICESTER

BLACKTHORN

RILL & LUDGERSHALL
DORTON

ASHENDON JC.

HADDENHAM
ILMER

PRINCES RISBOROUGH

SAUNDERTON

WEST WYCOMBE

HIGH WYCOMBE

BEACONSFIELD
SEER GREEN

DENHAM GOLF CLUB
DENHAM

WEST RUISLIP

GERRARDS CROSS

SOUTH RUISLIP

GREENFORD
PERIVALE
BRENTHAM

PARK ROYAL

OLD OAK LANE
WESTBOURNE PARK
ROYAL OAK

LONDON
PADDINGTON

line is joined by the Greenford Loop. This 2½-mile branch, opened in 1904, connects the new line with the GW main line at Ealing. As well as the local shuttle service between Ealing and Greenford the loop is regularly used by goods and parcels trains.

We are now running through the rapidly developing Middlesex suburbs; at Northolt, some 10 miles out from Paddington, stands the RAF aerodrome famous for its role during the Battle of Britain. From 1946 it was used as London's main civil airport, but lack of space saw development switched to nearby Heathrow, and in 1954 Northolt once again reverted to being a military establishment.

As we approach South Ruislip we are joined by the ex-Great Central line from Marylebone, which can be seen at a lower level, passing under our own line and then climbing alongside for about ½-mile to connect at South Ruislip station, which until 1932 had been named Northolt Junction. At this point we are now on the GW/GC joint section. South Ruislip is now served by both Marylebone suburban services and Central Line electric trains. As we pass through the station, notice the still unfinished Central Line station buildings. Between here and West Ruislip for a distance of about two miles we are running along a six-track formation. At West Ruislip the

Above:
In May 1956, Collett 'Hall' No 4977 *Watcombe Hall* **runs under the signal gantry at South Ruislip with the 4.10pm Paddington-Wolverhampton. To the right is the Central Line extension, and in the background the signalbox at Northolt Junction West.** C. R. L. Coles

Below:
On Sunday 2 September 1962 No 5008 *Raglan Castle* **takes water from Ruislip troughs as it heads the 6.10pm service from Paddington to Shrewsbury.**
M. Pope

Central Line terminates; notice the large electric train depot and sidings

Above:
Shovel power and human effort are well portrayed in this picture, as a 10-man permanent way team pack the ballast at Ruislip water troughs. C. R. L. Coles

Below:
Denham Golf Club halt in BR days. Opened on 22 July 1912, it was a typical GWR halt, provided with the minimum of facilities, pagoda waiting rooms and a couple of platform seats.
Lens of Sutton

here. Between here and Denham we pass over our first set of water troughs; situated on both up and down lines they extend for some 560yd. This gives an actual pick-up distance of 440yd, with some 60yd being allowed at either end for the lowering and raising of the scoop. Our engine should make its first water pick-up here. Once over the troughs we are soon joined by the 2½-mile branch from Uxbridge High Street. This was opened by the GWR on 1 May 1907, and although intended to link up with the branch from West Drayton to Uxbridge Vine Street, this was never completed. Passenger services were withdrawn as early as 1939, but the branch continues to be used by the occasional goods service. On the

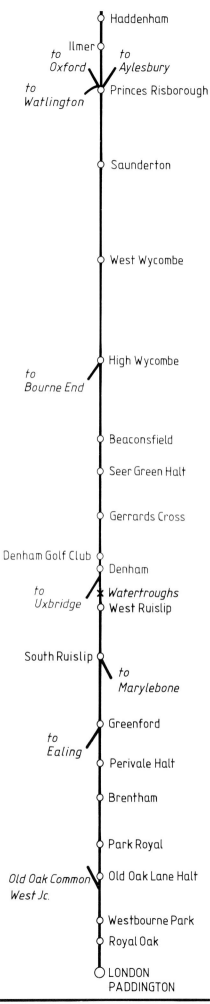

Haddenham
to Oxford — Ilmer — to Aylesbury
to Watlington — Princes Risborough
Saunderton
West Wycombe
High Wycombe
to Bourne End
Beaconsfield
Seer Green Halt
Gerrards Cross
Denham Golf Club — Denham
to Uxbridge — Watertroughs
West Ruislip
South Ruislip — to Marylebone
Greenford
to Ealing
Perivale Halt
Brentham
Park Royal
Old Oak Common West Jc. — Old Oak Lane Halt
Westbourne Park
Royal Oak
LONDON PADDINGTON

Above:
An unidentified 'King' on the 1.10pm Paddington-Birkenhead crosses the viaduct over the River Misbourne, between Denham Golf Club halt and Gerrards Cross on 27 December 1960. M. Pope

Right:
Gerrards Cross on 7 May 1960 with 'Large Prairie' No 6157 on the 12.38pm service from Princes Risborough to Paddington, whilst on the down platform the guard signals the right away for a Marylebone-High Wycombe service. The unusual two-storey station building can be seen behind the London-bound train. D. Trevor Rowe

approaches to Denham we pass over in quick succession, via two brick viaducts, the Grand Union Canal and the River Colne, as well as crossing the boundary from Middlesex into Buckinghamshire.

Holiday Haunts describes Denham as a 'remarkable village to find within easy reach of London, its sixteenth and seventeenth century houses are almost untouched'. Denham is also famous for its film studios, which are on the right just before entering the station. We are now starting to climb towards the Chiltern Hills, passing on the way the diminutive Denham Golf Club halt which because of its close proximity to Denham has been featured in many films. The gradient at this point is 1 in 175. The line now enters a series of deep chalk cuttings, the first of these is over 1½ miles in length. During its building some 1,228 cubic tons of chalk was removed. Situated in this cutting is Gerrards Cross station. Because of the deepness of the cutting at this point the main station building on the up platform is an unusual two-storey affair. Entrance to the station complex is via the upper level.

Still climbing, our train reaches the highest point on the line at Seer Green, some 315ft above sea level. The simple halt here serves the nearby Beaconsfield Golf Club. As we now start to drop down into Beaconsfield we once again pass through a series of chalk cuttings in one of which stands Beaconsfield station. The cutting depth here is some 85ft, the buildings here unlike Gerrards Cross, however, are of normal height. Entrance to the station complex is effected via a slip road cut into one side of the cutting, whilst a footbridge links the two platforms. Like both Denham and Gerrards Cross, Beaconsfield is a well built brick station and the four-track layout includes two platform loops.

Moving swiftly now we plunge into the 348yd-long White House Tunnel. During its construction in 1902 six navvies were killed by a roof fall. Once through the tunnel we pass Tylers Green signalbox before running over a high embankment and across the Penn Viaduct, 66yd in length, after which we enter the Wycombe Valley. Because of the terrain here the line had to be constructed along the

valley's edge. The town of High Wycombe can now be seen to good advantage across the Buckinghamshire Wye Valley. Shortly before arriving at High Wycombe, the only stop before Birmingham on our down journey, we are joined by the original Wycombe Railway route from Bourne End.

Standing some 26½ miles from Paddington and lying alongside the Chiltern beech woods, High Wycombe is arguably the country's most prolific and long established centre for furniture making. Famous for its Windsor chairs, production was such that during the latter half of the 19th century some 1¼ million of these were being produced here annually.

Here we join the earliest section of our line. The railway had reached High Wycombe on 1 August 1854 with the opening of a branch from Maidenhead. This broad gauge line was promoted by the Wycombe Railway Co in 1852 and on completion leased to the GWR at a fixed rent. It ran from a junction on the GWR Paddington-Bristol line at Maidenhead, for a distance of some 9¾ miles, to High

Wycombe. Extension of the line to Princes Risborough and Thame came on 1 August 1862 and to Kennington Junction near Oxford on 24 October 1864. The importance of High Wycombe as a rail centre was sealed with the opening of the GW/GC joint line on 2 April 1906 and secondly with the opening of the new GW cut-off

Left:
Ex-LNER 'L1' class 2-6-4T No 67778 waits to leave Beaconsfield with an afternoon service from Marylebone to High Wycombe. J. D. Edwards

Below:
Collett 'Castle' class 4-6-0 No 5010 *Restormel Castle* passes high above the furniture town of High Wycombe with the 6.45am service from Wolverhampton to Paddington on a sunny day in 1957. J. D. Edwards

route in July 1910. This latter section now put High Wycombe firmly on a GW main line. The opening of the earlier GW/GC section had seen much rebuilding in the area with the provision of a new station and yard here. Because of its cramped position alongside a hill, the platforms here are staggered and connected by a subway; the down side platform has a bay at the south end for the local services. Incoming goods traffic to the two small yards here comprise mainly of coal together with a considerable amount of wood for furniture production. Finished furniture also forms a good percentage of the outgoing goods traffic. Upwards of 100,000 tons of goods arrive and depart from High Wycombe each year; the considerable suburban, main line and goods traffic necessitates a large payroll, with employee numbers here approaching the 150 mark. The two-mile section between High and West Wycombe is controlled by four signal-boxes, Wycombe South, Middle, North and West, with Middle and South boxes open for 24 hours a day.

Leaving High Wycombe station (there is a 35mph speed restriction here) our train passes through a deep cutting, its main feature being the high level brick retaining wall, built of some 1¼ million Staffordshire Blue bricks. Winding our way along the hillside and passing the closed station at West Wycombe, we break out into open country. Here we can just glimpse on the left the Golden Ball on the top of West Wycombe Church which stands on the hillside above the notorious Hell Fire Caves. Running now through some delightful Chiltern country we approach the small intermediate station of Saunderton. Saunderton, some 32 miles from Paddington, was opened on 1 July 1901 and in typical railway fashion stands some three miles from the village it serves. It comprises just two platforms, with the main station buildings situated on the down side. The single goods siding to the north of this platform is controlled by Saunderton signalbox which stands opposite on the up side. Just beyond the station the line crosses the Icknield Way, an ancient British trackway.

About a mile or so northwards from Saunderton the up and down lines diverge for about 2½ miles. Originally a single line at this point, doubling took place during 1905 with the provision of a new up line. The old single line had a rising gradient of 1 in 88 in the up direction, so when the new up line was constructed the gradient was eased to 1 in 167 by way of a deep cutting and an 84yd tunnel, with the old formation being retained as the new down line. Shortly before entering Princes Risborough the up and down lines once again converge. For the next seven miles to Haddenham we are on a falling gradient of between 1 in 88 and 1 in 200. High speed running is the norm on this section.

Some 34½ miles from Paddington is Princes Risborough. Standing under the shadow of the nearby Chiltern Hills, Princes Risborough took its distinctive title from its association with the Black Prince, and the site of his moated palace can still be seen nearby. The railway came to Princes Risborough with the opening on 1 August 1862 by the Wycombe Railway Co of its branch from High Wycombe to Thame. On that same date a small station was opened here. On 24 October 1863 the same company had extended its territory with the opening of a 7½-mile branch as far as Aylesbury. Extension of the original Wycombe Railway route from Thame to Kennington Junction was duly completed on 24 October 1864, thus bringing Princes Risborough on to a through route from Oxford and the North. Originally built as broad gauge lines, both were soon converted to standard gauge, Risborough-

Aylesbury in October 1868, Risborough-Kennington Junction during August 1870.

The next stage in the growth of the railway at Princes Risborough came with the opening on 15 August 1872 by the Watlington & Princes Risborough Railway Co of an 8½-mile

Far left:
The incredible brick retaining wall containing some 1¼ million Staffordshire blue bricks can be seen to good effect as 'King' No 6008 *King James II* winds its way out of High Wycombe with the 2.10pm service from Paddington to Birkenhead on 14 May 1959. H. Harman

Above:
What a magnificent sight No 6007 *King William III* makes as it accelerates past Wycombe North yard with the down 'Inter-City' service to Wolverhampton. J. D. Edwards

Above left:
No 6029 *King Edward VIII* heads a down express through the delightful Chiltern countryside at Saunderton. F. J. Saunders

Left:
The neat and tidy appearance of a small country station is reflected by Saunderton, here photographed in the mid-1950s. The signalbox can be seen at the north end of the up platform, as can the small yard opposite. Lens of Sutton

Left:

The up 'Cambrian Coast Express', formed of British Railways Mk 1 carriages, heads through Saunderton cutting hauled by No 6016 *King Edward V* on a sunny day in July 1962. M. Pope

Bottom:

The wonderful sight of a 'Castle' at speed is seen here as No 5072 *Hurricane* screams through Princes Risborough with the 7.40am service from Birkenhead to Paddington on 4 November 1961. At this point it is about to start the 1 in 264 climb towards Saunderton as the gradient post to the right shows. B. Jennings

an enormous affair containing a 98-lever frame and it stands within the junction of lines at the north end of the station. Passenger traffic was withdrawn from the Watlington branch on 1 July 1957; with only four services each way per day the effect on the overall passenger traffic was minimal. The line still remains open for goods traffic, also serving the large cement works at Chinnor. As our train hurries through Princes Risborough the line to Aylesbury can be seen to the right, whilst on the left what appears to be a double track formation is in fact two single line branches running parallel to each other, one to Watlington, the other to Thame and Oxford.

Some three miles north of Princes Risborough we pass a small halt at Ilmer, which was built by the GWR in 1929 to supplement the autotrain service between Banbury and Risborough. We now run over a series of embankments before entering a cutting; here we pass the station at Haddenham, again an elaborate affair for the size of the village it served. Haddenham signalbox stands to the north of the down platform. As with many other stations on the new line, passing loops are also provided here. Shortly after leaving Haddenham our train crosses over the River Thame by way of the 220ft-long Chearsley Viaduct. Through the Buckinghamshire countryside we soon arrive at Ashendon Junction. Here the ex-Great Central and Great Western joint line curves away to our right to Grendon Underwood, where it joins the ex-Great Central main line from Marylebone to Leicester. The signalbox here stands to the south of the junction between the up and down tracks.

branch between these two points. With the amount of traffic being created by these three routes, train working must have been very interesting at this time, for the line south of Risborough was still a single-track formation.

For the opening of the joint line in 1906 a new station was provided here. A new up platform contained a bay at either end, together with a new entrance, booking hall, and waiting rooms. A footbridge connected this platform to the down platform which was of an island type, this also was provided with a bay at the northern end. Platform loops were constructed to allow for fast through running. A prominent feature here is Princes Risborough North signalbox; this is

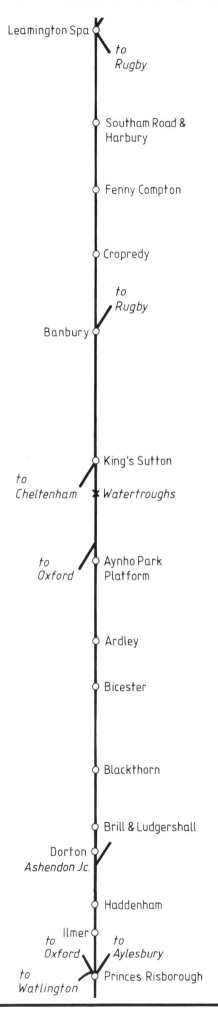

The 'Inter-City' was not always 'King'-hauled, as this May 1956 picture clearly illustrates. 'Castle' No 5008 *Raglan Castle* approaches the summit at Saunderton with the up 'Inter-City'. Judging by the amateur-looking headboard, the engine could well be deputising for a failed 'King'.
C. R. L. Coles

Ashendon Junction itself was opened together with the new cut-off route in 1910, the flying junction on the up GW line here allows a junction speed of some 60mph. From now until Aynho we are on the cut-off route which incidentally was the last main line to be built in this country. Shortly after leaving Ashendon we pass Dorton halt; opened on 26 June 1937 it is one of the halts on the line that is served by the regular auto service from Banbury to Princes Risborough. Shortly before entering the 191yd Brill Tunnel we pass under the track-bed of the now closed Brill Tramway. This outpost of the Metropolitan Railway was opened in 1872 and ran from nearby Brill to Quainton Road where it connected with Great Central main line, and Metropolitan Railway services to London and the North. It was closed to passengers in 1935.

Emerging from the tunnel we pass through Brill & Ludgershall station, unstaffed since 1956 and now designated a halt, although it still retains all of its buildings and goods sidings. Approximately one mile north of Brill we move from Buckinghamshire into Oxfordshire, passing the remains of Blackthorn station. This was one of the many fine stations built for the new line, but little used, being closed as early as 1953; no passing loops were provided here. From Blackthorn the line is carried for the next three miles on various embankments on the approaches to Bicester. Just before arriving at Bices-

ter North, our route passes over the ex-LNWR line from Oxford to Bletchley. This was opened by the LNWR under the auspices of the Buckinghamshire Railway Co from Bletchley to here by 1850 and throughout on 20 May 1851. Bicester's other station, Bicester London Road, is situated on this line.

Bicester is the largest town on the cut-off route and has always been an important town in Oxfordshire, with at one time a flourishing market; early guidebooks refer to it being noted for its fine lace and good ale. The main station buildings here can be seen on the down side and once again are brick built; the two-platform formation also includes two through running lines, with the whole four-track layout spanned by a footbridge. The station yard contains numerous sidings and a large goods shed. The whole of the station site is situated on a large embankment overlooking the town. It was the building during World War 2 of a large ordnance depot that was to bring added prosperity to the town. Although served by rail by the nearby Oxford-Bletchley route, many army personnel used the services to and from the ex-GW station. Some idea of the size of this complex can be gleaned from the fact that it contains nearly 40 miles of track. The influx of workers and service staff after it was completed in 1940 effectively doubled the population of the town.

Leaving Bicester we now enter the last stretch of the cut-off route. The

line continues for some way along an embankment before we start the 1 in 200 climb up to Ardley, where once again we enter a cutting. As we pass through Ardley, we can see yet another fine brick-built station com-

Below:
Standing in the middle of the Buckinghamshire countryside was Ashendon Junction. On 27 August 1955 the former streamlined 'King' No 6014 *King Henry VII* speeds across the GC line on its way to Paddington with a morning service from Wolverhampton. S. Creer

Right:
Repairs to both the track and the flyover bridge at Aynho Junction are in evidence as No 6003 *King George IV* approaches with the 8.30am fast service from Paddington to Wolverhampton on 23 April 1960. The lower level tracks of the original route to Birmingham via Oxford can just be seen behind the trees. R. C. Riley

Below right:
On 31 May 1960, No 4907 *Broughton Hall* is seen collecting the slip coach from the 5.10pm Paddington-Wolverhampton service at Bicester North. The coach is then added to the 4.34pm semi-fast service to Wolverhampton, which is waiting in the station. The Bicester slip was the last slip coach working in the country, finally coming to an end on 9 September 1960. M. Mensing

plete with through running lines. The various sidings here serve the nearby limestone quarry. We now run through yet another cutting before entering Ardley Tunnel, at 1,147yd the longest on the line. On leaving the tunnel we enter the Cherwell Valley and for a short time North-amptonshire.

Travelling high above the valley across the two Souldern Viaducts (No 1 is 580yd, No 2 some 400yd long) we pass the small halt at Aynho Park, opened on 1 July 1910. To the left at a lower level is the line from Oxford to Birmingham, together with Aynho's

Top:
'Castle' class No 5087 *Tintern Abbey* speeds through the closed station at Blackthorn with the 12.10pm Paddington-Wolverhampton. This station was the first on the cut-off route to be closed, passenger services being withdrawn on 8 June 1953. R. C. Riley

Above:
This fine view of a 'King' in the Northamptonshire countryside shows No 6021 *King Richard II* as it climbs away from the Cherwell Valley across the viaducts at Souldern with a London-bound service on 28 October 1961. Dr G. Smith

Above right:
The 2.40pm Birkenhead-Paddington hauled by No 6016 *King Edward V* takes the up line, on to the cut-off route at Aynho Junction on 29 August 1962, just a few weeks before 'King' class engines were withdrawn from the route.
M. Mensing

Right:
The lovely stone station at Kings Sutton can be seen behind No 5026 *Criccieth Castle*, as it makes its way southwards with the 'Pines Express' on 27 May 1963. The 'Pines' was re-routed via Birmingham and Oxford from 9 September 1962. Dr G. Smith

other station, Aynho for Deddington. Here we join the Oxford line by means of a flying junction; crossing the Oxford line via a box girder bridge, we descend past Aynho Junction signalbox to the junction itself. We are now on the original Oxford & Rugby Railway route.

Between here and Kings Sutton lie Aynho water troughs, again some 560yd in length. A second water pick-up will be made at this point. At Kings Sutton the Banbury and Cheltenham line from Kingham runs in from the left. Opened in 1887 it was closed to passengers between Banbury and Chipping Norton on 4 June 1951, the short life of the line being reflected by a passenger who had travelled on the first train and was also able rather sadly to travel on the last. Kings Sutton station itself was opened in 1872 and unlike the brick-built stations of the cut-off route is built in local stone. To the north of Kings Sutton lies Twyford Mill; there has

been a mill on this site since the time of the Norman Conquest.

Passing now into open country we are at this point still in Northamptonshire. The Oxford Canal and River Cherwell, only a few hundred yards away to our left, are actually both in Oxfordshire, such is the closeness of our line to the division between these two counties. In fact we shall re-enter Oxfordshire just prior to our arrival at the market town of Banbury. We are now 67½ miles from Paddington and approximately halfway on our journey to Wolverhampton. As we enter Banbury we are joined by a single line running in from our right. This is the ex-LNWR branch from Verney Junction, opened on 1 May 1850, which runs parallel to our own before terminating at Banbury Merton Street.

We pass in quick succession the locomotive depot at Banbury opened in 1908 and to our right Banbury gasworks, opposite which is situated Banbury South signalbox. We now enter the newly constructed station at Banbury. Banbury is perhaps best known for its famous Cross and Banbury cakes, but it has equal commercial importance firstly for the distribution of ironstone from the many quarries locally and secondly as a centre for the sale of livestock. Banbury livestock market, situated behind the nearby Merton Street station, is one of the largest in the South of England. Many of the animals are conveyed in special livestock trains to and from the market.

As already mentioned, the LNWR arrived at Banbury in 1850. It was soon followed by the GWR under the auspices of the Oxford & Rugby Railway Co, who duly opened a station at Banbury on 2 September 1850. Initially Banbury had two terminal stations, for, when opened, the Great Western station was for a while the

northern terminus of the proposed broad gauge route from Oxford to Rugby. However, by the time the line was extended northwards in 1852, the Rugby portion had been dropped in favour of a more direct route to Birmingham from Fenny Compton via Leamington. It was also opened throughout as a mixed rather than a broad gauge-only line.

The station at Banbury today is rather different to that originally provided; this was a wooden structure containing an overall roof in typical Brunel style, and was known for a while as Banbury Bridge Street. Initially provided with just two platforms, which at the time were quite adequate, in order to cope with the increase in traffic from the newly opened Great Central line at Banbury Junction these platforms were extended during 1903, with the added provision of bays at either end. For the opening of the cut-off route in 1910 further improvements were undertaken with the addition of new station buildings to provide better passenger and parcels facilities; however, the original wooden structure and overall roof still remained.

A decision had been made by the GWR during 1938 to rebuild the station completely. However, due to the intervention of World War 2 this was never undertaken. The old station soldiered on, almost intact, until for safety reasons the overall roof was removed during 1952. In fact for many years prior to this act, drivers were advised to take extreme care whilst passing under the overall roof due to the unsafe nature of the structure. It was not until 1956, under the British Railways Modernisation Plan, that a start was made on replacing the old station. This was duly completed during 1958 and gives us the layout that we can see today. Entrance to the two island platforms

Above:
Standing adjacent to Banbury General was the ex-LNWR terminus at Merton Street, seen here in 1957. Opened in 1850, it was eventually closed to passengers on 31 December 1960.
J. D. Edwards

Right:
No 6011 *King James I* passes Cropredy on the northernmost outskirts of Oxfordshire with the 4.10pm Paddington-Birkenhead service on 14 August 1952. Cropredy was one of the first stations on the route to be closed, succumbing on 17 September 1956.
R. H. G. Simpson

is effected by a large overbridge, which also carries a refreshment room and offices. The up platform is provided with two bays, one at either end. The north bay is generally used by the incoming Woodford local services, whilst the south bay is almost exclusively used by auto-train services to Princes Risborough. The down platform contains two through running lines with a central bay at the north end, this is mostly used by the outgoing local services to Woodford. An interesting feature of the new station is the provision of large electric clocks at either end of the platforms.

Leaving Banbury we pass under the large roadbridge that carries the main A361 road to Daventry over both the railway and the River Cherwell that can now be seen once again to our left

behind Banbury North signalbox. This box controls the entrance and exit to the large goods yard situated opposite. Passing the yard, rows of guards' vans can be seen standing on a small hump siding awaiting their attachment to the many goods trains that both start and terminate here. This yard now follows us all the way to Banbury Junction, a distance of over one mile. The original two smaller yards were combined in 1931 by the addition of many new sidings to form the much larger 2,000-wagon capacity Banbury New Hump yard.

Again improvements and additions during World War 2, particularly on both sides of the main line at Banbury Junction, have left us with the massive goods yard that we can see today. At Banbury Junction the ex-GC line to Culworth Junction and Woodford Halse diverges away to the right in a northeasterly direction. Standing opposite on the left are the ironstone sidings which feed the privately-owned Oxfordshire Ironstone Co.

At Cropredy we pass the remains of the small station that was closed to passengers in 1956. Not far from here

Above:

In the spring of 1961, 'Modified Hall' No 6987 *Shervington Hall* passes Fenny Compton with an up parcels train. The platforms at this station were staggered, the up platform being situated behind the photographer. W. Turner

Left:

No 6021 *King Richard II* climbs Fosse Bank between Leamington and Harbury with the up 'Cambrian Coast Express' on 14 February 1961. F. A. Haynes

at Cropredy Bridge during 1644 was fought one of the major battles of the Civil War when the Roundheads suffered a major defeat by the Royalists. Once past Cropredy we leave Oxfordshire, and moving onwards through the Warwickshire countryside we arrive at the interesting junction station at Fenny Compton. To the south of the station we pass under the Stratford-upon-Avon & Midland Junction line from Towcester to Stratford, opened by that company on 1 June 1871. It closed to passenger traffic in April 1952. At one time

Fenny Compton possessed two stations, the GWR and the SMJR at Fenny Compton West, standing side by side but on two different lines. On our right we are joined once again by the Oxford Canal. The small basin here was once used for an exchange of goods between the canal and the railway. For the next few miles the countryside opens out, and looking to the southwest the horizon is dominated by Edge Hill, the scene, in 1642, of yet another Civil War battle.

Approximately five miles beyond Fenny Compton stand Greaves' Sid-

ings and signalbox. The sidings here feed the adjacent cement works. The last intermediate station between Banbury and Leamington is Southam Road & Harbury, a simple two-platformed affair standing in a deep cutting. Also situated in this cutting is Harbury Tunnel which at just 73yd in length is the shortest on our journey. Once leaving the tunnel we soon pass Fosse Road goods loop and signalbox, which was opened in 1950 and replaced an earlier box that was situated opposite on the down side. For the next few miles we are on a falling gradient of 1 in 187 which eases as we approach Leamington. Passing over a series of bridges and viaducts we enter the town of Leamington Spa. The small ex-GWR locomotive depot can be seen on the right, sandwiched between our own line and the incoming ex-LNWR branch from

Rugby. Dominating the skyline as we approach the station is the parish church of All Saints, Leamington, reputed to be one of the six largest parish churches in the country. Leamington has long been famous for its spa waters, and a visit by Queen Victoria in 1838 designated Leamington as a Royal Spa town. Acknowledged as the 'green heart of England' (an oak within the town boundary supposedly marks the traditional centre of England), Leamington is also a centre for commerce and tourism; the town itself contains many fine shops. Urban spread has meant that nearby Warwick has now almost become part of Leamington itself. Tourism brings

many seasonal visitors to Leamington, both to see the town and the nearby Warwick Castle, whilst many travellers by rail change trains here to travel to nearby Stratford-upon-Avon.

Leamington is well served by the railway. Adjacent to the ex-Great Western station stands Leamington Spa Avenue; this ex-LNWR station has services from both Coventry and Rugby and was opened in 1854. The Oxford & Birmingham Railway opened its own station here in 1852. With the general increase in services over the years the station has undergone a series of improvements, many of which were undertaken between 1890 and 1910 when the station was

enlarged and platforms lengthened. Just prior to World War 2 the GWR station was completely rebuilt which resulted in the fine station that we can see today. Entrance to the up island platform is effected by a subway, thus the down platform contains most of the station offices, together with a fine buffet restaurant. The bay at the north end of this platform is mainly used by trains to Stratford-upon-Avon. Two central through lines allow non-stop running through the station, although the sharp curve at the south end has a speed restriction of 40mph.

Leaving Leamington our train passes the large 121-lever Leamington North signalbox, behind which we can

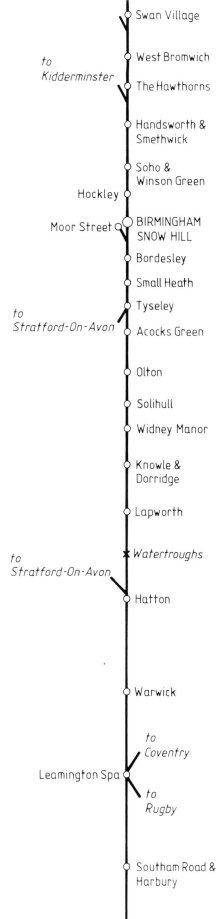

Swan Village

to Kidderminster

West Bromwich

The Hawthorns

Handsworth & Smethwick

Soho & Winson Green

Hockley

Moor Street

BIRMINGHAM SNOW HILL

Bordesley

Small Heath

to Stratford-On-Avon

Tyseley

Acocks Green

Olton

Solihull

Widney Manor

Knowle & Dorridge

Lapworth

Watertroughs

to Stratford-On-Avon

Hatton

Warwick

to Coventry

Leamington Spa

to Rugby

Southam Road & Harbury

Fenny Compton

see the ex-LNWR branch from Leamington Avenue to Coventry moving away to our right. We now start to drop down a short 1 in 101 bank towards Warwick, passing under the Grand Union Canal, which crosses over our line by way of an aquaduct, and almost immediately we also cross the River Avon before tackling the steepest climb on our route. For the next six miles we shall climb to Hatton with the major gradient running for three miles at 1 in 103/105. Warwick station is situated near the start of the climb, and one banking engine is usually kept here, although we shall not need it; as we speed through we can just see to our left the

historic tower of Warwick Castle. Between here and the top of the bank at Hatton a slow line is provided on the down side.

At Budbrooke we are joined once again by the Grand Union Canal. It was here in 1800 that the Warwick & Napton met the Warwick & Birmingham Canal to form a new route into London. Both were subsequently incorporated into the Grand Union during 1929. Over the next two miles the canal has a combined rise/fall of some 146ft, which is achieved by the provision of no less than 21 locks.

The locomotive is now working very hard, and soon we reach the summit of our climb, Hatton station, where the

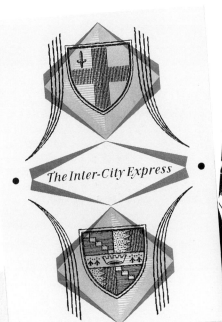

Below:
Almost there! No 6015 *King Richard III* nears the summit of Hatton Bank with the down 'Inter-City' on 25 October 1955. The fitting of double chimneys, blastpipes and four-row superheaters on these majestic engines gave the whole class a new lease of life. No 6015 was the first to be so fitted, being converted during September 1955.
M. Mensing

Bottom:
The 11.10am Paddington-Birkenhead climbs Hatton Bank behind 'Castle' No 5044 *Earl of Dunraven* on 12 January 1957. T. E. Williams

line to Bearley and Stratford-upon-Avon leaves ours, its triangular junction being seen to our left. The large building that now comes into view on our right is Hatton Psychiatric Hospital; the large chimney of its boiler house is a prominent feature of the skyline here. Quite soon after passing through Hatton we start to enter the southern suburbs of Birmingham. At Rowington we will make yet another water pick-up as we pass over the third set of water troughs since leaving London. The junction of the Henley-in-Arden railway was situated here; this small 3½-mile-long branch was opened to passengers by the Birmingham & Henley-in-Arden Railway Co, together with the GWR,

Top left:
2-6-2T No 5185 arrives at Hatton station with a three-coach Leamington Spa-Moor Street service in April 1957.
Real Photos (K3370)

Above:
The up 'Cambrian Coast Express' hauled by No 7032 *Denbigh Castle* is diverted to the slow line at Lapworth on 29 April 1957, owing to the relaying of both up and down main lines.
R. H. Short

Left:
Standard '9F' 2-10-0 No 92250, fitted with a Giesl ejector, trundles over Lapworth troughs with an up part-fitted freight for Banbury yards on 20 September 1961. M. Mensing

on 6 June 1894. A short-lived line, it closed to passengers on 1 January 1915 and completely on 1 January 1917. Between here and Lapworth we also cross the Stratford-upon-Avon Canal, which was opened in 1816. At Lapworth station we enter a four-track formation that continues right through to Birmingham. Quad-rupling of the section between Lap-worth and Olton was completed during May 1933. Over 30 bridges were widened and many of the stations were either rebuilt or enlarged. From Lapworth northwards all intermediate stations are provided with platforms on both the main and relief lines.

For many years before the war, Lapworth had been served by slip coaches, as many as three a day. The section here is reasonably flat, so allows for some fast running; between here and Tyseley the line runs through many cuttings. We pass rapidly through the stations at Knowle & Dorridge and Widney Manor, the latter being opened during 1899. Solihull, one of the larger towns on the south Birmingham commuter

belt was yet another station once served by slip coaches. Soon after passing Olton and Acocks Green, two stations that are only a mile apart, we are joined at Tyseley by the North Warwickshire line from Stratford.

Tyseley is one of the newer stations on our route, being opened for passengers on 1 October 1906 in anticipation of the North Warwicks line which was opened just a year later. Similar in style to several others in the area, the entrance to the four platforms is gained via the roadbridge above. There are many sidings here on both sides of the track, those on the left being the carriage and DMU sidings for the Birmingham suburban traffic.

Passing by, we can also glimpse the large engine shed here. It was opened during June 1908 and supplies much

Above far left:
No 6003 *King George IV* restarts the 3.10pm Paddington-Wolverhampton from Solihull station on 30 May 1960. The quite extensive goods sidings here can be seen behind the 5.05pm Birmingham Snow Hill-Swansea service which is formed of two Cross-country diesel sets. M. Mensing

Far left:
Super power for the up 'Inter-City' as 'Castles' Nos 5043 *Earl of Mount Edgcumbe* and 5001 *Llandovery Castle* pass through Olton on 26 September 1961. The extra locomotive was probably needed as the train loading on this day had been increased to 12 coaches. M. Mensing

Top:
Mogul No 6349 arrives at Acocks Green & South Yardley with the 6.05pm Birmingham Snow Hill-Leamington service on 21 April 1960. M. Mensing

Left:
A Moor Street-Leamington service hauled by 2-6-2T No 5163 arrives at the beautifully clean and tidy Acocks Green & South Yardley station on a sunny day in March 1957. Real Photos (K3316)

Left:
Standard Class 5 No 73014 runs through Tyseley station on 30 August 1958 with the 8.30am Pembroke Dock-Birmingham Snow Hill. M. Mensing

Below left:
The up 'Cambrian Coast Express' passes Tyseley behind 'Castle' No 5089 *Westminster Abbey* **piloting 'King' No 6015** *King Richard III* **on Saturday 30 August 1958.** M. Mensing

Bottom left:
The majority of the '6100' class 2-6-2Ts operated in the London area. A few, however, were allocated to Tyseley for Birmingham suburban workings. One such engine, No 6166, is seen here at Small Heath & Sparkbrook with the 4.50pm service from Snow Hill to Lapworth on 30 March 1957.
M. Mensing

Above:
The attractive entrance to Small Heath & Sparkbrook station in the early 1950s. Its Great Western pedigree can still be clearly seen with the painting out of the word 'Great' on the wooden name-board. Lens of Sutton

Below:
A fine picture of a 'King' at speed, as No 6013 *King Henry VIII* **on the down 'Cambrian Coast Express' storms through Bentley Heath on 27 December 1960.** M. Mensing

Above:
No 6831 *Bearley Grange* approaches Tyseley with a down goods. The 127-lever signalbox here, when opened on 1 October 1906 was the largest in the Birmingham area.   M. Mensing

Right:
The Saturdays-only Wolverhampton-Paignton service crosses the 797yd-long Bordesley Viaduct, as it leaves the city of Birmingham on its journey southwards. Motive power is provided by a 'Hall' class 4-6-0.   J. C. Flemons

Above far right:
'Castle' No 4085 *Berkeley Castle* emerges from Snow Hill Tunnel with an up parcels service on 12 November 1960. The train is just passing over the ex-LNWR lines to New Street.
M. Mensing

Far right:
One of the through workings via the North Warwicks line was the 9.10am ex-Kingswear, seen here at Birmingham Moor Street on 3 September 1960. The train engine, No 5946 *Marwell Hall* of Exeter shed, having finished its duty is moving off the locomotive traverser. It will now run back to Tyseley shed to be serviced.   M. Mensing

of the motive power for the local suburban and goods traffic. The 127-lever signalbox at Tyseley was opened on 1 October 1906 and at the time was the largest in the area. We are now only 2½ miles from Snow Hill. Standing between Small Heath & Sparkbrook and Bordesley stations, and situated on either side of the track, are the large goods yards at Bordesley Junction. In the downside yard once stood Bordesley engine shed, replaced in 1908 by the new engine shed that we have just passed at Tyseley. At the north end of the up

yard is the junction with the Midland Camp Hill line that runs between Kings Norton and Saltley. At Bordesley station we are now well and truly in the city of Birmingham. As we cross the 797yd-long Bordesley Viaduct on our approach to Snow Hill Tunnel, a derelict viaduct can be seen curving away to our right; this is Duddeston Viaduct some 50 chains in length. Built in the early 1850s by the GWR to connect the Birmingham & Oxford line to the nearby Grand Junction terminus at Curzon Street, it was never used and was abandoned

shortly after the line opened to Snow Hill in October 1852. On our left is Moor Street station.

A station at Moor Street had been proposed as early as 1894 by the Birmingham & North Warwickshire Railway Co, but when building was eventually started in 1908 it was by the GWR. This company had absorbed the Birmingham & NWR Co and provided the capital for the new station which was opened for services on 1 July 1909. A two-platform terminus, engine release was rather unusually achieved by the provision of

a pair of locomotive traversers, which were situated at the terminus end of the station. A general increase in traffic on the line saw the station enlarged by the provision of a further two platforms. A large goods shed together with various sidings were provided here during 1914.

Although primarily a suburban station for the North Warwickshire area, the station regularly sees much summer excursion traffic, for which it is useful in that the traversers are capable of accommodating 'Castle' class engines. A long running regular

summer service from here is the 7.30am Saturdays-only Moor Street-Paignton; after passing Moor Street we plunge into Snow Hill Tunnel. This was extended in 1874 and is now 596yd in length. One interesting feature of the tunnel is the 1 in 45 rising gradient for trains entering from the South. We emerge to enter one of the most charismatic of the ex-Great Western Railway stations, Birmingham Snow Hill. This station started with humble beginnings, for when the line was opened through from Oxford on 1 October 1852 only a

temporary wooden station was provided. This structure, basically a large wooden shed, housed three platforms and two through lines, and at the time of opening passenger services terminated here. Snow Hill became a through station with the opening of the line northwards to Wolverhampton in 1854. The name Snow Hill seems to have been adopted from about 1858, as before this date it was known as either Livery Street or Great Charles Street.

By the time the broad gauge was removed in 1869 proposals were at hand to rebuild the station. This

Left:
The clock shows 2.00pm exactly as No 6930 *Aldersley Hall* arrives at Snow Hill with 9.11am Portsmouth Harbour-Wolverhampton through service on 22 August 1959. M. Mensing

Below left:
For several days in 1959 a 5mph PW slack outside the southern entrance to Snow Hill Tunnel involved the double-heading of many down trains. On 2 May of that year the 2.10pm Paddington-Birkenhead arrives at Snow Hill behind No 6008 *King James II* and pilot Standard Class 4 No 75026. The pilot engine was attached at Leamington and removed at Snow Hill. M. Mensing

Bottom left:
On 16 August 1958, Churchward Mogul No 6361 in immaculate lined green livery runs back through Snow Hill with the empty stock of the 8.50am service from Margate to Birmingham. The engine had arrived about three-quarters of an hour previously with the train, before running round at Queens Head in preparation for its return working to Tyseley carriage sidings. M. Mensing

Right:
The Author's favourite locomotive, No 5012 *Berry Pomeroy Castle* gains admiring glances as it waits to leave Snow Hill on the 9.30am service from Bournemouth West to Birkenhead on 1 April 1961. M. Mensing

Below right:
Youthful spotters admire No 6935 *Brownsholme Hall* as it prepares to leave Snow Hill with the 5.45pm service to Stratford-upon-Avon and Worcester on 16 April 1960. M. Mensing

subsequently took place during 1871, the old wooden station being removed to Didcot, where it was subsequently re-erected as a carriage shed. The new station, although adequate, was hardly one of the Great Western's more notable achievements. The layout of the station was constructed around two main platforms, each approximately 600ft in length. Smaller bay platforms were provided at the north end. The whole complex was connected by a large footbridge that also spanned two through running lines. Offices, waiting and refreshment rooms were provided on both up and down platforms. The centre portion of the station was covered by a large glazed roof which had a span of some 92ft. Entrance to the station could be effected from either Snow Hill or Livery Street. In 1863 the Great Western Hotel was opened at Colmore Row. Built at road level it spanned the south end of the station, but lack of patronage saw it close in 1909. The GWR then converted the building into office accommodation for goods and station administration, although a public

restaurant was still retained on the ground floor.

Birmingham was designated a city in 1889, but even before this date the population was expanding rapidly, with the resulting increase in usage of the railway systems. By the turn of the century some 400 trains per day were using Snow Hill, and because of the inability of the existing facilities to handle this amount of traffic, a decision was made by the Great Western once again to rebuild the station. Work started in September 1906, but because of its cramped position with main thoroughfares on either side and a tunnel at the south, sideways expansion was difficult, therefore most of the enlargement of the station complex was undertaken northwards.

The new layout was on the island platform principle, entered via a new booking and entrance hall that was constructed above the platform level in Colmore Row. The two island platforms were extended to some 1,200ft in length, each containing two bay platforms at the north end. The downside bays were initially provided with a sector table for locomotive release but this gradually fell out of use and was removed in 1938. As with the earlier station, both platforms were provided with all of the main services, offices, waiting and refreshment rooms and public toilets, but now greatly expanded on the previous facilities. The whole complex was covered by a series of glazed roofs, the main section of which covered an area of 12,000sq yd. As each of the main platforms was long enough to accommodate two trains at once, these were allocated two separate platform numbers, giving Snow Hill a total of 12 platforms.

A feature of Snow Hill was the provision of a new Siemens electric signalling system, one of the first to be used on the GWR. This was controlled from the large signalbox at the north end of the station. The box, containing some 224 levers, was opened for operation on 31 October 1909. A smaller 96-lever box at the south end of the station was opened shortly after the station rebuilding was completed in 1913. Both are currently still in use, although a new panel box is now being constructed on the down platform. When complete it will replace both of the old boxes. This rebuilding was the last major work to be carried out at the station, although bomb damage during World War 2 necessitated repairs to the overall roof together with several of the buildings. Since the war Snow Hill has become one of the busiest stations on the system, particularly during the summer months when many hundreds of extra holiday trains are run.

It is now time to depart once again on the final lap of our journey to Wolverhampton. This last 12½-mile stretch will take us into the heart of the industrial Midlands, an area known worldwide as the 'Black Country'.

Moving slowly out of Snow Hill past the large signalbox and Northwood Street carriage sidings we enter two tunnels, the 132yd-long Hockley No 1 and the 160yd Hockley No 2. Emerging from the tunnels we pass on our left the large goods depot at Hockley, before accelerating away through the station; here we enter a four-track formation that continues as far as Handsworth. Just ¾-mile beyond

Left:
The up 'Cambrian Coast Express' hauled by No 6016 *King Edward V* runs through a rather run down-looking Soho & Winson Green on 25 November 1961. M. Mensing

Below left:
The PW man seems transfixed as No 6011 *King James I* rushes past with the 8.55am Birkenhead-Paddington on Friday 22 June 1956. The train is just approaching Handsworth & Smethwick station. M. A. Walker

Below:
The 1.10pm service from Paddington to Birkenhead is seen climbing through The Hawthorns halt hauled by No 6005 *King George II* on 25 March 1961. This halt, opened in December 1931, was used by football excursions to the nearby West Bromwich Albion ground.
M. Mensing

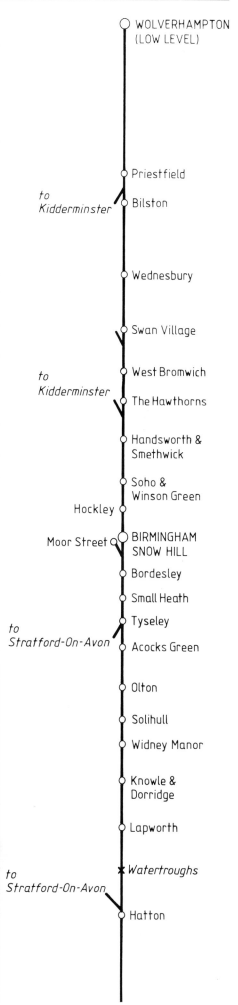

'King' No 6020 *King Henry IV* hauling the 7.30am Shrewsbury-Paddington, storms through West Bromwich station on 20 September 1958.   M. Mensing

The 4.35pm stopping train from Stourbridge Junction and Dudley hauled by Mogul No 6340 arrives at West Bromwich on its journey to Birmingham Snow Hill. The train then forms the 6.05pm service to Leamington. The date is 17 September 1958.   M. Mensing

Above:
No 6866 *Morfa Grange* is seen on an up semi-fast service passing Swan Village on 3 August 1957. The unusual style of the station buildings can be seen to good advantage. M. Mensing

Left:
Collett 'Grange' class 4-6-0 No 6828 *Trellech Grange* takes the Dudley line at Priestfield with a Wolverhampton-Worcester service in June 1957. The ex-GW route from Wolverhampton to Birmingham Snow Hill can be seen running away to the right.
Real Photos (K3436)

Hockley stands the station at Soho & Winson Green. It has five platforms and yet another large goods depot. Here also our own line is crossed by the ex-LNWR line from Soho to Perry Barr. At Queens Head on the approaches to Handsworth & Smethwick is yet another large goods yard, controlled by Queens Head signalbox situated on our left. Moving through the yard we almost immediately enter Handsworth & Smethwick station.

The entrance to the six-platform layout is situated on the up side. Its imposing building is built of brick and stone in the classic style; a similar style is also used at Wednesbury, West Bromwich and Bilston stations. Standing on the left between here and Handsworth Junction is the large factory of the Birmingham Carriage & Wagon Co, builders of locomotives and rolling stock for use in both this country and abroad.

At Handsworth Junction the line to Old Hill and Stourbridge diverges away to the left. The rather derelict-looking platforms that we can see here are in fact the Hawthorns halt, opened in December 1931. It is nowadays generally only used on match days when the nearby West Bromwich Albion football club is playing at home. We are now back on a double-track formation; at West Bromwich notice once again the elaborate station buildings provided here. Approaching Swan Village we can see on our left the disused colliery at Sandwell Park, before passing under a brick bridge that carries a cable operated tramway from the nearby Jubilee colliery to a sorting and distribution area away on our left.

Above:

'Castle' class 4-6-0 No 5047 *Earl of Dartmouth* leaves Wolverhampton Low Level with the 11.10pm Paddington-Birkenhead on Saturday 12 September 1959. M. Mensing

Right:

0-6-0PT No 3778 attaches extra stock including a refreshment car to the rear of the 8.50am Birkenhead-Paddington at Wolverhampton Low Level on Whit Monday 11 June 1962. The High Level station and viaduct can be seen in the background. Note also the cramped position of the signalbox against the retaining wall here. M. Mensing

At Swan Village the triangular platform layout of the station serves both our own line and also that to Great Bridge and Dudley that runs away to the left. Swan Village station is unusual as its buildings are constructed mainly of wood and are certainly not in keeping with the other stations on the line. Crossing over the Birmingham Canal we soon enter Hill Top Tunnel, some 412yd in length, emerging to see the town of Wednesbury in the distance; the three spires of St John's, St Mary's and St Bartholomew's Churches are prominent on our right. Arriving at Wednesbury we cross, via a girder bridge, the ex-LNWR route from Dudley to Walsall. Notice the extensive yards here that supply the various steel and chemical works situated nearby. Crossing the canal once again we approach Bilston, passing on our left the disused site of Willingsworth colliery. Bilston is another heavily industrialised town, a major centre for iron and steel production; many of the factories in this area are associated

with these products. The large steel works of Stewarts & Lloyds is also situated here, its foundries supplied with iron ore from the Oxfordshire Field. Once past Bilston the country opens out. At Priestfield we pass through yet another triangular station, the line joining us from the left is the original OW&WR route from Dudley to Wolverhampton opened in 1854. The tight curve of our own line through the station to the junction necessitates a 30mph speed restriction. Passing Stow Heath signalbox we are rapidly approaching Wolverhampton; on our left here is Walsall Street goods depot, behind which and running in at a higher level is the ex-LNWR Stour Valley line from Birmingham New Street to Wolverhampton High Level. This now runs parallel with our own line into Wolver-

hampton; we however enter the Low Level station through a 377yd-long twin-bore tunnel, which itself passes under the Wryley & Essington Canal. Emerging from the tunnel we arrive at our journey's end: Wolverhampton, the largest town in Staffordshire.

The station at Wolverhampton Low Level was opened on 14 November 1854. A joint station, it was served by no less than three different railway companies — the Oxford, Worcester & Wolverhampton, the Great Western and the Shrewsbury & Birmingham. In the years before the turn of the century, the station, which had started off as a single-platform affair, had been gradually enlarged by the addition of a new up platform and bay. In 1899 extensive track remodelling took place to incorporate a large carriage shed and new through goods

Above:

Double chimney-fitted 'King' No 6015 *King Richard III* prepares to leave Wolverhampton Low Level with the up 'Inter-City' on Friday 1 September 1961. Standing on the through line with an empty stock train is No 5944 *Ickenham Hall*. Dr G. Smith

Below:

Shown here is 0-6-0PT No 3776 minus cabside number plates, preparing to move a rake of carriages from the carriage shed at Wolverhampton Low Level. By this date, April 1965, all main line services from Wolverhampton to Paddington were diesel-hauled. Mike Soden

lines. During the 1920s the large overall roof of the station was removed, leaving the station very much as we can see it today.

All of the main buildings and offices are situated on the down side. The main entrance and booking hall is built in brick and stone in the classic style and provides a fine frontage to what is essentially quite a small station. The two main platforms can hold up to 12-coach trains and local services run from the bays that are situated at each end of these platforms. Wolverhampton Low Level is a busy station with many through services changing engines here.

Through goods trains now use the loop lines that run between the up platform and the carriage sidings.

As we leave our train, it is well worth reflecting that we have travelled 123 miles in a little over 2½hr from the suburbs of London through the Chiltern countryside, across the undulating fields of Oxfordshire and Warwickshire right into the heart of the industrial Midlands. The carriages will be taken away and cleaned and serviced in preparation for the return trip to London, whilst our engine and crew will run up to Wolverhampton Stafford Road shed for a well-earned rest.

2
Passenger Services

The completion of the new line brought to the Great Western the ability to compete with the LNWR for the lucrative London-Birmingham services. Prior to its opening, the best the GWR could achieve was a point-to-point time of some 2hr 20min for the 129½ miles via Oxford. The LNWR route from Euston to Birmingham was only 113 miles in length, and that alone ensured that the GWR would always have to take second best. All of this was to change with the opening of the cut-off section from Ashendon to Aynho in 1910. At 110½ miles, the GWR now had the shorter route, and with the introduction of the 1910 summer timetable, took on the LNWR, with the immediate introduction of two-hour express services.

Whereas the LNWR route to Birmingham is relatively flat, the Great Western route is of an undulating nature with several climbs and various speed restrictions, notably at High Wycombe and Leamington. These early services were in the hands of 'Saint' and 'Star' class 4-6-0 engines, and admirably though they performed on these 2hr trains, the increased loadings required something more powerful. The GWR provided the answer in 1928 with the introduction on to the line of the new 'King' class engines; at the time the most powerful engines in the country. The 'Kings' were to transform express passenger working on the line, for not only were they able to easily maintain a 2hr schedule, they were able to do it with greatly increased loads. Such was the performance of these locomotives that a regular 'King' turn, the 9.10am from Paddington to Birkenhead, was able to pick up at High Wycombe and still maintain a 2hr schedule. This, however, was the exception rather than the rule, as it was impossible to do this at other important stations en

Left:
Seen pulling away from a 15mph speed restriction at Hatton is the 6.30am service from Birkenhead to Paddington, hauled by 'Castle' No 5047 *Earl of Dartmouth* on 19 March 1955.
T. E. Williams

Below:
'King' class No 6006 *King George I* makes a fine spectacle as it climbs Hatton bank on the 4.10pm Paddington-Birkenhead (the reporting number should read 187) on 29 April 1957.
T. E. Williams

Above:

An immaculate No 6011 *King James I* storms up Hatton Bank with the 1.10pm Paddington-Wolverhampton service on 26 April 1962. The apparent excellent condition of the engine belies the fact that it was withdrawn just eight months later. Dr G. Smith

Right:

The slip coach from the 5.10pm Paddington-Wolverhampton service is seen here braking at Bicester North station. It will be attached to the 4.34pm Paddington-Wolverhampton semi-fast, the last coach of which can be seen to the left of the picture. The photograph dates from 25 August 1960. M. Mensing

Below:

Youthful 'spotters' admire double chimney-fitted 'Castle' No 5022 *Wigmore Castle* as it departs from Wolverhampton Low Level with the 4.20pm service to Paddington on Friday 1 September 1961. Dr G. Smith

route without incurring a severe time penalty. The GWR cleverly provided the answer to this problem by the extensive use of slip coaches on the line.

Bradshaw's Guide of 1914 showed no fewer than 19 slip workings between Paddington and Birmingham. These were as follows: five for Leamington Spa, five for Banbury, three for Hatton, two for Warwick, and one each for Bicester, Knowle, Lapworth and Princes Risborough. Some of these were multiple slip workings: the 4.00pm from London, for example, slipped coaches at Bicester, Leamington Spa and Knowle, with the 6.05pm slipping at Banbury, Leamington Spa and Lapworth.

Slip coach working was suspended during both world wars: it was, however, when the service was resumed after the second conflict that the decline of slip working on the line became apparent with only two workings remaining, the first being the 5.10pm down Wolverhampton, which slipped at Bicester at 6.15pm, the slip coach was then attached to the 6.34pm stopping train to Banbury. The second train was the 7.10pm down Wolverhampton which slipped two coaches at Princes Risborough at 8.06pm, this latter service being on Fridays and Saturdays only. By 1958 only the Bicester slip remained, becoming ultimately the only slip working in the country, until it also was withdrawn from the timetable, the very last slip taking place on 9 September 1960 at approximately 6.12pm.

In the years before World War 1, fast running was the order of the day on the new route, with six up and seven down 2hr runs. These, together with the slip services already mentioned, provided a service on the route that was second to none. After World War 1, extensive revamping of the GWR timetables set a standard departure time for the down services of 10min past the hour, with up trains timed to report from Birmingham on the hour.

By the early 1930s the non-stop runs had all but disappeared from the route, many of the workings now including stops at High Wycombe, Banbury and Leamington. During this time the crack train on the route, as far as locomotive handling was concerned, was the 6.10pm down service to Birkenhead, worked by a Stafford Road 'King' as far as Wolverhampton. The addition of two slip coaches for Bicester and Banbury would regularly give this train a starting load of some 500 tons. Allowing for a stop at Leamington the train was timed at 90½min for the 87½ miles between these two points: a further 26½min was allowed for the run to Snow Hill. When one considers the gradient profile of the route together with the unavoidable speed restrictions, it required first-class performances from both man and machine. By 1938 there were 14 through trains daily on the route but with the outbreak of war in 1939 these were reduced to just eight.

The end of hostilities brought a great increase in passenger usage on the line: one such train that saw this

increased patronage was the 9.10am express from Paddington to Birkenhead. It was soon apparent that a relief train was needed and subsequently, on weekdays only, a 9.00am relief restaurant service was incorporated into the timetable. Stopping at High Wycombe only, it reached Birmingham in just 2hr, countinuing to Wolverhampton where it arrived at 11.25am. During October 1950 it was bestowed with the title the 'Inter-City'. The up service left Wolverhampton at 4.35pm, and with stops at Birmingham, Leamington and High Wycombe reached the capital at 7.10pm.

Motive power was usually provided by a 'King' class locomotive supplied by Old Oak Common for both the up and down services. Loading initially

was in the form of eight coaches which were strengthened to nine on Mondays and Fridays by the addition of another first. In November 1959 the daily loading was increased to 11 coaches. An interesting comparison of the 1951 and 1959 loadings can be seen below:

This increased loading also meant a deceleration of the times, with a 13min increase in the schedule time between Paddington and Birmingham, arrival now being at 11.13am, Wolverhampton being reached at 11.40am. Compensation was provided with a new non-stop restaurant ser-

9.00am (SX) Paddington-Wolverhampton: the 'Inter-City'

1951	1959
1 Brake Third	1 Brake Second
3 Thirds	4 Seconds
1 Diner	1 Second Restaurant & Kitchen
2 Firsts*	1 Open First Restaurant
1 Brake Composite	3 Firsts
	1 Brake Composite

* Three Firsts Monday and Friday.

Left:
No 7019 *Fowey Castle* climbs the 1 in 75 section of Wilmcote Bank soon after leaving Stratford-upon-Avon, with a summer Saturday holiday train to Wolverhampton in August 1964.
M. Pope

Above:
Seen on the southern approaches to Stratford-upon-Avon on 16 August 1958 is the 10.35am Paignton-Wolverhampton service powered by No 4980 *Wrottesley Hall*. In the adjacent goods loop stands 'Large Prairie' No 5163 on a freight.
Brian Morrison

Right:
The superb sight of a 'King' in full cry as No 6005 *King George II* blasts its way up Saunderton Bank with the 6.10pm Paddington-Shrewsbury on 20 July 1961. M. Pope

Table 12

THE INTER-CITY
RESTAURANT CAR SERVICE

LONDON, BIRMINGHAM and WOLVERHAMPTON

WEEK DAYS
(Mondays to Fridays)

	am			pm
London (Paddington) .. .. dep	9A 0	Wolverhampton (Low Level).. dep		4B35
High Wycombe .. .. .. ,,	9 36	Birmingham (Snow Hill) .. ,,		5B 0
		Leamington Spa General .. ,,		5 28
Birmingham (Snow Hill) .. arr	11 13	High Wycombe .. .. .. arr		6 39
Wolverhampton (Low Level) ,,	11 40	London (Paddington) .. .. ,,		7 15

A—Seats can be reserved in advance on payment of a fee of 2s. 0d. per seat (see page 23).

B—Except for 22nd and 29th July, seats can be reserved in advance on payment of a fee of 2s. 0d. per seat (see page 23).

Above left:
The summer 1960 'Inter-City' timetable. Author's Collection

Above:
From the beginning of the winter timetable in 1962, main line services between Wolverhampton and Paddington were hauled by the newly introduced 2,700hp Type 4 'Western' class diesel-hydraulics. Shortly before the complete dieselisation of the services No D1004 *Western Crusader* in green livery passes Bentley Heath with the 4.30pm service from Birkenhead to Paddington 12 July 1962. M. Mensing

Right:
The temporary withdrawal of the 'Kings' with bogie problems saw two 'Princess Royal' 4-6-2s loaned to Stafford Road to help cover the gap. One of these, No 46210 *Lady Patricia* is seen here leaving Snow Hill on 8 February 1956 with the 11.45am Birkenhead-Paddington service. M. Mensing

vice which left Paddington at 8.30am arriving at Birmingham at 10.30am and Wolverhampton at 10.55am. This train took over the mantle from the 'Inter-City' as the fastest train on the line. Until September 1962 these services were still in the hands of 'King' class locomotives. At that date the 'Kings' were withdrawn *en bloc* and replaced with the new Type 4 'Western' class diesels. The impact was immediate, with many of the trains being rescheduled to cover the 110 miles from Paddington to Birmingham, including various stops en route, in just 2hr.

Considerable disruption to the services took place on the line in the mid-1950s, firstly by locomotive problems and secondly by major rebuilding and repair work. Problems with the front bogies of the 'Kings' required a temporary withdrawal of the class for remedial work to rectify this

problem. For a short while 'Castles' filled the gap, but during May 1956 two ex-LMS 'Princess Royal' Pacifics, Nos 46207 *Princess Arthur of Connaught* and 46210 *Lady Patricia* were allocated on a temporary basis to Stafford Road to help cover this crisis. They were diagrammed to work the 9.10am down service from Paddington and 2.35pm up service from Wolverhampton.

In 1956 the rebuilding of Banbury station caused a certain amount of disruption, but as most services called here at this time, delays were minimal. It was between May 1957 and October 1957 that the most serious disruption of services took place, when it was found that urgent repairs were required to both Souldern viaducts. Since the opening of the cut-off route, these structures had given little trouble, but now severe problems with the supporting masonry necessitated

'King' class No 6013 *King Henry VIII* storms under the road bridge, as it reaches the summit of Saunderton Bank with the 7.40am Birkenhead-Paddington on 13 January 1962.
B. Jennings

urgent repairs that required single-line working. At times this caused considerable hold-ups, even though schedules had been decelerated by between 5 to 10min to allow for the rebuilding work.

During 1956/57 all of the 'Kings' were fitted with double blastpipes, double chimneys and four-row superheaters. These modifications gave a new lease of life to a class that was nearly 30 years old.

The table below shows a run with one of the newly modified 'Kings': No 6011 *King James I* of Wolverhampton Stafford Road on the 8.00am up service from Snow Hill to Paddington. Although leaving on time, four out-of-course signal checks, together with PW restrictions at Banbury station (rebuilding) and Souldern viaducts (repair work) should have resulted in a late arrival at Paddington, but excellent work by both locomotive and crew ensured an arrival some 4½min inside the scheduled time.

Above:
Hawksworth 'County' No 1005 *County of Devon* approaches the top of Wilmcote Bank with a Bristol-Birmingham football excursion on 16 February 1957. T. E. Williams

8.00am Birmingham Snow Hill-Paddington

Locomotive: No 6011 *King James I* (84A)
Load: 11 coaches, 377 tons tare, 405 tons gross

Miles		min/sec	mph
0.0	Birmingham	0.00	—
3.3	Tyseley	5.43	—
		signal stops	—
7.0	Solihull	16.11	54/63
10.4	Knowle	20.06	—
2.5	Lapworth	4.29	65
6.3	Hatton	8.32	60/75
10.9	Warwick	12.04	70*
12.9	Leamington	14.20	—
3.7	Fosse Road	6.20	54
6.1	Southam Road	9.10	59/67
11.0	Fenny Compton	13.46	66/64
16.2	Cropredy	18.05	80
19.9	Banbury	21.09	50*
24.9	Aynho Junction	26.09	70
		pws	10*
30.1	Ardley	34.44	49/69†
33.9	Bicester	38.22	63*
39.9	Brill	43.24	78
43.2	Ashendon Junction	46.21	60*
		52.31	sig
47.2	Haddenham	53.42	stop
52.6	Princes Risborough	62.11	51/48
55.8	Saunderton	65.53	63
58.5	West Wycombe	68.37	50*
60.7	High Wycombe	71.30	35*
65.6	Beaconsfield	76.30	64
69.9	Gerrards Cross	80.04	83
72.5	Denham	81.52	92
77.0	South Ruislip	84.52	90
83.4	North Acton	89.13	—
84.0	Old Oak Common West Junction	90.21	35*
		signal stop	—
87.3	Paddington	100.50	—

* Speed reduced.
† At Ardley summit.

The above table by Dr D. S. Bailey is reproduced from the August 1956 *Trains Illustrated* magazine with kind permission from Ian Allan Ltd.

Although the bulk of the traffic on the line was concentrated on the Paddington-Wolverhampton section, we must not forget that many services continued northwards to and from Birkenhead. Prior to the opening of the cut-off route, Birkenhead was reached via Oxford. One such train was the 'Birmingham and North Corridor Express' which left Paddington at 2.10pm arriving at Birkenhead Central at 7.45pm, slipping a coach en route at Leamington. Connections were made at Birkenhead and Liverpool with the various boats to and from Ireland, trains being timed accordingly.

The opening of the new route saw many of these through services switched to this line. The tradition of boat trains continued into the 1930s with the running of a 'Belfast Boat Express' from Paddington, which connected with the Belfast service at Liverpool, leaving London at 4.10pm to connect with the evening sailing; the up service left Birkenhead at 9.05am. After Nationalisation much of this boat traffic was switched on to the ex-LMS lines via Liverpool. Through running continued to Birkenhead however with the 1951 timetable showing five down and five up services per day; by 1959 this total had risen to six each way. Services continued almost unaltered until the general rundown of the lines in the mid-1960s; the last through service between these two points taking place on 4 March 1967, aptly steam hauled by (now preserved) 'Castle' class No 7029 *Clun Castle*.

Being a great promoter of holiday lines it was no real surprise that the Great Western take-over of the Cambrian lines in 1923 resulted in the provision of both through coaches and through trains on a regular basis. Even before the Grouping the GW had run a summer Saturdays holiday train on the route via Shrewsbury to Aberystwyth and Pwllheli; leaving Paddington at 9.50am it was known as the 'Cambrian Coast Express'. After the Grouping the train was retimed to leave Paddington at 10.20am, dividing at Wolverhampton into sections for Birkenhead and Aberystwyth. However, after 1924 the train settled down to a daily 10.10am departure time, which by 1927 had become a summer Saturday-only working once again. Arrival at Wolverhampton was at 12.44pm where an engine change took place, with the train running non-stop to Welshpool via the Abbey Foregate curve, thus avoiding Shrewsbury. At Welshpool another engine change took place and the train ran on to Dovey Junction where it was divided into portions for Pwllheli and Aberystwyth, the latter being reached at 3.55pm. The up service left Aberystwyth at 11.45am. In the last summer before the outbreak of World War 2 the departure time once again was altered back to 10.20am.

Once the war was over the service was soon restored, and by 1954 became a daily restaurant car service once again, with a 10.10am departure time. A headboard was now provided bearing the title 'Cambrian Coast Express'. The train now stopped at Banbury en route, running from Wolverhampton direct to Shrewsbury where engines were exchanged and reversal took place; Aberystwyth being reached at 4.05pm. Coaches for Pwllheli were now detached at Machynlleth. The up service left Aberystwyth at 11.15am. Interestingly the Saturday service left Paddington at 10.15am and ran direct from Wolverhampton to Welshpool just as it had before World War 2. By the summer of 1960 the departure time was once again altered to 11.10am, to accommodate the new 'Birmingham Pullman' diesel service that had been introduced during that year. Motive power during the latter years of steam traction was in the hands of either 'King' or 'Castle' 4-6-0 locomotives as far as Shrewsbury, with the smaller 'Manor' class 4-6-0s or BR Standard '4MT' 4-6-0s providing motive power on the Cambrian sections. By the end of 1963 the 'Cambrian' was being

diesel-hauled as far as Wolverhampton, from here to Shrewsbury it still used steam traction in the shape of Oxley-allocated 'Castles', 'Halls' and 'Granges'. As with the rest of the through services on the line, the 'Cambrian Coast Express' ceased to run after 4 March 1967.

From the opening of the cut-off route, main line passenger services had changed little over the ensuing 40 years with an average of eight through services each way daily between Paddington and Wolverhampton. However, the decision to electrify the route between Euston and Wolverhampton was to have a profound effect on the services using the cut-off route. Firstly it provided an Indian Summer of express running, and then once completed it signalled the end of the through services. Electrification work was started during 1959 and very soon many of the Euston to Wolverhampton services were diverted on to the cut-off route,

Right:
Some interesting double-heading as 2-6-2T No 8100 pilots No 5018 *St Mawes Castle* through Widney Manor station with the 8.50am Margate-Birmingham service on 28 September 1960.
M. Mensing

Bottom:
The 'Cambrian Coast Express' timetable for summer 1960.
Author's Collection

giving a daily service of 15 down and 14 up trains, still retaining departure times of 10 minutes past the hour from Paddington, and on the hour from Birmingham. Many of these trains were now very heavily loaded, often being strengthened to 12- and 14-coach formations. Obviously extra motive power was needed and to facilitate this almost the whole of the 'King' class was allocated to the line, with Stafford Road having 11 and Old Oak Common 16.

Table 13

CAMBRIAN COAST EXPRESS
RESTAURANT CAR SERVICE (¶)
LONDON, ABERDOVEY, TOWYN, BARMOUTH, PWLLHELI and ABERYSTWYTH

WEEK DAYS

	E am	S am
London (Paddington) .. ..dep	10A10	10A10
Banbury General .. .. { arr	11 28	11 35
{ dep	11 30	11 38
	pm	pm
Birmingham { arr	12 24	12 31
(Snow Hill) { dep	12 28	12 35
Wolverhampton { arr	12 48	12 57
(Low Level) { dep	12 54	1 4
{ arr	1 29	..
Shrewsbury { dep	1 33	..
..arr	2 11	2 22
Welshpool .. .. .. ,,	2 40	3 0
Newtown.. .. .. .. ,,	2 49	..
Moat Lane Junction .. .. ,,	3 30	3 46
Machynlleth .. .. .. ,,	3 45	4 0

	E	S
Machynlleth.. .. ..dep	3 45	4 0
Penhelig Halt .. ..arr	4 5	4 19
Aberdovey .. .. .. ,,	4 8	4 25
Towyn .. .. ,,	4 16	4 32
Tonfanau .. .. .. ,,	4 21	..
Llwyngwril .. .. .. ,,	4 32	4 46
Fairbourne .. .. .. ,,	4 40	4 55
Morfa Mawddach .. .. ,,	4 44	4 59
Barmouth .. .. .. ,,	4 50	5 5
Dyffryn-Ardudwy .. .. ,,	5 3	5 19
Harlech.. .. .. .. ,,	5 17	5 32
Penrhyndeudraeth .. .. ,,	5 29	5 43
Portmadoc .. .. .. ,,	5 38	5 52
Criccieth .. .. .. ,,	5 50	6 10
Afon Wen .. .. .. ,,	5 56	6 18
Penychain B .. .. .. ,,	6 0	6 23
Pwllheli .. .. .. ,,	6 10	6 33

	E	S
Machynlleth .. .. ..dep	3 35	3 52
Dovey Junction .. ..arr	3 41	..
Borth .. .. ,,	3 55	4 15
Aberystwyth .. .. .. ,,	4 15	4 35

	E am	S am
Aberystwyth .. ..dep	9A45	9A45
Borth .. .. ,,	10A 5	10A 5
Dovey Junction .. .. ..arr	10 21	10 22

	E	S
Pwllheli .. ..dep	7A40	..
Criccieth .. .. .. ,,	8A 3	..
Portmadoc .. .. .. ,,	8A14	..
Penrhyndeudraeth .. .. ,,	8A23	..
Harlech .. .. ,,	8A42	..
Llanbedr and Pensarn .. ,,	8 50	..
Dyffryn-Ardudwy .. .. ,,	9 0	..
Barmouth .. .. .. ,,	9A20	..
Morfa Mawddach .. .. ,,	9A27	9A20
Fairbourne .. .. .. ,,	9A30	9A23
Llwyngwril .. .. .. ,,	9A39	9A32
Towyn .. .. ,,	9A53	9A48
Aberdovey .. .. .. ,,	10A 0	9A56
Penhelig Halt .. .. .. ,,	10 3	10 1
Dovey Junction .. .. ..arr	10 17	10 17

	E	S
Dovey Junction .. .. ..dep	10A28	10A39
Machynlleth .. .. .. ,,	10A37	10A39
Moat Lane Junction .. .. ,,	11 22	11 25
Newtown.. .. .. .. ,,	11 31	11 34
	pm	pm
	12 7	12 10
Welshpool { arr	12 42	..
{ dep	12 50	..
Shrewsbury { arr	1 27	1 29
{ dep	1 34	1 36
Wolverhampton { arr	1 56	1 56
(Low Level) { dep	2 0	2 0
Birmingham { arr	2 24	2 26
(Snow Hill) { dep	2 26	2 29
Leamington Spa General		
London (Paddington) .. ..arr	4 0	4 20

A—Seats can be reserved in advance on payment of a fee of 2s. 0d. per seat (see page 23).
B—For Pwllheli Holiday Camp.
E—Except Saturdays.
S—Saturdays only.
¶—Restaurant Car available between London (Paddington) and Aberystwyth, in each direction.

Up Services

Time		Destination	Depot		Load
6.30am		Birkenhead	Stafford Road		11
6.45am	SX	Wolverhampton	Stafford Road		11
7.25am		Wolverhampton	Stafford Road	SX	12
			Old Oak	SO	11
7.30am		Shrewsbury	Stafford Road		12
7.35am		Birkenhead	Stafford Road		12
8.55am		Birkenhead	Stafford Road		11
9.45am†		Aberystwyth	Old Oak		9
11.40am		Birkenhead	Old Oak		11
2.20pm	FO	Wolverhampton	Stafford Road		10
2.35pm		Birkenhead	Old Oak		11
3.33pm	SX	Wolverhampton	Old Oak		9
4.20pm	SX	Wolverhampton	Stafford Road		9
4.30pm		Birkenhead	Old Oak		12
4.35pm*		Wolverhampton	Old Oak		11

Down Services

Time		Destination	Depot		Load
8.30am		Wolverhampton	Old Oak		9
9.00am*	SX	Wolverhampton	Old Oak		11
9.10am		Birkenhead	Old Oak		11
10.10am†		Aberystwyth	Old Oak	SX	
		Pwllheli	Stafford Road	SO	9
11.10am		Birkenhead	Stafford Road	SX	
			Old Oak	SO	11
1.10pm		Birkenhead	Old Oak		12
2.10pm		Birkenhead	Stafford Road		12
3.10pm		Wolverhampton	Old Oak		9
4.10pm		Birkenhead	Stafford Road		12
5.10pm	SX	Wolverhampton	Stafford Road		13
6.08pm	FO	Wolverhampton	Old Oak		10
6.10pm		Birkenhead	Stafford Road		11
6.23pm		Wolverhampton	Stafford Road		11
7.10pm	SX	Wolverhampton	Old Oak		9
8.10pm		Shrewsbury	Stafford Road	SX	11
			Old Oak	SO	11

* The 'Inter-City'
† The 'Cambrian Coast Express'

Allocation of 'King' class locomotives for Paddington-Wolverhampton services, April 1960

Old Oak Common 6000/3/4/9/10/12/15/18/19/21/23/24/25/26/28/29
    Total: 16
Stafford Road 6001/5/6/7/8/11/14/17/20/22/27
    Total: 11

As already mentioned the service was supplemented by the introduction of a new diesel Pullman service. The 'Birmingham Pullman', as it was known, was a six-car set powered at each end by a 1,000hp diesel unit. Daily workings were introduced leaving Wolverhampton at 7.00am, with a London arrival at 9.30am. It returned at 10.10am running now only as far as Birmingham, and returned to London at 2.55pm before finally forming the 4.50pm down service back to Wolverhampton. This service was also a casualty when through services were withdrawn in 1967.

From its opening in 1908 the North Warwickshire line has provided an important through route from the Midlands to the South. Soon after its opening the GW were running through trains from Wolverhampton to Penzance and from Birkenhead to Bristol. Between the wars, services were being run between Wolverhampton and Birmingham to Bristol, Cardiff, Plymouth and Penzance. South Wales was particularly well served with through trains to Cardiff, Swansea and Carmarthen. On 9 July 1934 a new express diesel railcar service was introduced over the route, running between Birmingham and Cardiff in only 2 hr 20min, calling only at Gloucester and Newport en route. Many of the long-distance through trains ran on summer Saturdays only, the timetable for 1938 showing no fewer than 12 of these each way.

World War 2 saw all of these services over the line suspended. Once hostilities were over, through services were gradually reinstated and by the early 1950s were back to pre-war levels. In 1952 a new-named express appeared on the North Warwicks line when the 9.15am Wolverhampton-Penzance through service was officially named the 'Cornishman'. The 'Cornishman' was the name that had originally been used in 1890 to

describe the 10.15am from Paddington to Penzance, a forerunner of the 'Cornish Riviera Express'.

The new 'Cornishman' left Wolverhampton at 9.15am and arrived at Snow Hill at 9.50am. From here it proceeded along the GW main line as far as Tyseley, where it took the North Warwicks line to Stratford-upon-Avon, and then travelled via Cheltenham and Bristol arriving at Penzance at 5.55pm. Permanent way diversions quite often saw this train travel via Hatton North Junction and Bearley. From 10 September 1962 the 'Cornishman' was re-routed away from the Western Region and on to the Midland route, via Birmingham New Street and Gloucester.

In 1957 the Western Region introduced a new buffet car service between Birkenhead and Cardiff. Departing from Birkenhead at 7.50am, the return working left Cardiff at 4.15pm. Motive power was usually provided by a 'Hall' class engine. During 1957 DMU trains were introduced on to some of the South Wales services and by 1958 had taken over all of these workings. Steam still reigned supreme on the West of England holiday trains, running to destinations such as Paignton, Penzance, Weston-super-Mare and Minehead. For a good number of years, in order to avoid congestion at Snow Hill, several of the services to

and from Penzance, St Austell and Paignton were operated from Moor Street.

The route to Stratford-upon-Avon from the south via Leamington and Hatton had always been served by through carriages, at the turn of the century by coaches slipped at Leamington. The opening of the new route was to provide an even faster service from Paddington to Stratford-upon-Avon. Many summer-only trains were run between these points, mainly, of course, to exploit the tourist trade. The 'Shakespeare Express' was a feature of the 1928 timetable; a through service from Paddington to Stratford-upon-Avon, it left Paddington at 9.25am,

and with stops at High Wycombe, Leamington and Warwick, Stratford was reached at 11.33am. For a time this service also slipped a coach at Banbury en route. The up departure left Stratford at 5.30pm, thus allowing some six hours to explore 'Shakespeare Land'. Even a motor coach tour was organised in conjunction with the service to take in some of the other attractions of the area. The name was resurrected once again during the Festival of Britain in 1951, when the 10.10am Paddington-Wolverhampton carried through coaches for Stratford. These were detached at Leamington, and the service then carried the name 'William Shakespeare'.

Top:
'Castle' No 5079 *Lysander* leaves the Birmingham-Stratford line at Bearley North Junction, on the single line section to Bearley East Junction with the diverted 3.20pm Wolverhampton-Paddington on 24 May 1959.
T. E. Williams

Right:
'The Cornishman' hauled by 'Castle' No 5047 *Earl of Dartmouth*, tops the bank at Wilmcote on the last leg of its journey over the North Warwicks line on 15 June 1957. M. Mensing

Intermediate and Local Services

To discuss the local services on the route it is necessary to divide the line into three separate sections, for this is the way these services were actually operated.

Section (i): Wolverhampton-Birmingham-Stratford-Leamington

Section (ii): Leamington-Banbury-Princes Risborough

Section (iii): Princes Risborough-High Wycombe-London

Top:
One of two '8100' class 'Large Prairie' 2-6-2Ts allocated to Leamington Spa depot (84D), No 8109 stands in the down bay with a Leamington-Stratford service on a sunny August day in 1952.
Brian Morrison

Right:
The 8.50pm to Worcester waits to leave Leamington Spa General behind Standard 2-6-2T No 82030 on Sunday 9 August 1959. This service will travel via Stratford-upon-Avon and Honeybourne. M. Mensing

Within the framework of the main line traffic the GWR and latterly the Western Region operated an extensive network of suburban services within the Birmingham area. The opening of Moor Street, together with the North Warwicks line, saw a gradual spread of population to these outlying areas. The provision of new stations on the route southwards to Leamington saw a gradual encroachment of the population, turning small villages into the outer suburbs of Birmingham. The GWR answered this growth in traffic

with a gradual programme of improvements to both track and stations. Between 1908 and 1933 the 13 miles of track between Moor Street and Lapworth were quadrupled, 33 bridges were widened and many stations were either replaced or enlarged. Leamington Spa, the southern terminus for many of the outer suburban services, was itself rebuilt during 1936. Even the North Warwicks line saw some improvements with the opening of halts at The Lakes and Whitlocks End during 1935 and 1936 respectively.

Apart from the upheaval of the two world wars, services changed little over the years. Extra trains at peak hours provided almost a half-hourly service on the Leamington/Snow Hill/ Moor Street route, with a similar frequency to both Wolverhampton and Stratford-upon-Avon. However, off-peak the service was spasmodic with sometimes a two-hour wait between

trains. After World War 2 this problem was gradually tackled with additional services being run at off-peak times. It was to take the Western Region to bring a measure of standardised working into the suburban network, and during 1954 they undertook an extensive revision of the local passenger services in the Birmingham and Wolverhampton area. The final result was to give a regular interval service together with standard departure times. First introduced for the 1954 winter timetable, they were as follows:

North Warwicks line: Birmingham-Stratford-upon-Avon
An hourly service between 9.10am and 9.10pm from Moor Street to Henley-in-Arden or Stratford-upon-Avon, with additional semi-fast services operating between Snow Hill and Stratford-upon-Avon.

Stratford-upon-Avon-Birmingham
An hourly service between 9.20am and 9.20pm from Henley-in-Arden and Stratford-upon-Avon to Moor Street, with semi-fast services between Stratford-upon-Avon and Snow Hill.

Birmingham-Leamington

Hourly 8.50am-9.50pm between Snow Hill and Knowle & Dorridge. Also

Below:
The 2.50pm service from Snow Hill to Lapworth arrives at Tyseley hauled by 0-6-0PT No 3664 on 29 August 1959.
M. Mensing

Bottom:
The 5.38pm Birmingham Snow Hill-Knowle & Dorridge passes Bentley Heath crossing on the final stage of its journey on the evening of 28 April 1959. Motive power is supplied by 2-6-2T No 4172. M. Mensing

hourly from 10.20am to 10.20pm between Moor Street and Leamington Spa.

Leamington-Birmingham

Hourly 10.00am-10.00pm between Leamington Spa and Moor Street. Also hourly 9.53am-9.53pm from Knowle & Dorridge to Snow Hill.

Wolverhampton Low Level-Birmingham Snow Hill

Hourly service 9.10am-10.10pm, calling at all stations except during off-peak times.

Birmingham Snow Hill-Wolverhampton Low Level

Hourly service 5.30am-10.30pm, calling at all stations except at off-peak times.

The service to Stratford-upon-Avon was also supplemented with extra trains between here and Leamington Spa. All of these at this time were still steam-hauled: however from 1957 extensive use was made of newly introduced diesel multiple-units, and by the early 1960s steam had all but disappeared from the Birmingham suburban scene.

Between Leamington and Banbury the three intermediate stations of Southam Road and Harbury, Fenny Compton and Cropredy were served by the local Leamington to Banbury trains together with some through stopping services between Wolverhampton and Oxford. At the turn of the century this gave a daily service of five trains per day each way with an additional train on Thursdays (market day), a frequency that was to continue until well after Nationalisation. By 1953 the frequency had dropped to four a day each way on weekdays only. Cropredy station was closed on 11 September 1956; the two remaining intermediate stations now only had three services a day. Closure of these remaining stations took place on 2 November 1964, which saw the stopping service disappear for ever between Banbury and Leamington.

The stations and halts on the new cut-off route were catered for by a stopping service between Banbury and Princes Risborough. Inaugurated soon after the line was opened in July 1910, the service was operated on the auto-train principle, so popular with the GWR. Initial services saw five of

Top:
The 6.05pm Birmingham Snow Hill-Leamington Spa leaves Olton on 6 July 1961 behind No 7824 *Ilford Manor*.
M. Mensing

Above right:
'4300' class Mogul No 6367 arrives at Acocks Green station with the 6.05pm stopping service from Snow Hill to Leamington on 20 July 1959.
M. Mensing

Right:
Ex-GW diesel railcar No W15W stands at Snow Hill on 28 August 1958 with an afternoon service to Dudley.
C. A. Keevil

these trains per day call at the seven intermediate stations between Banbury and Princes Risborough. In order to increase the patronage the GW opened two further halts on the cut-off route at Ilmer in 1929 and Dorton in 1937. This service continued almost unchanged until January 1963.

Bicester, the one large town between Banbury and Princes Risborough, was also served by various semi-fast services that either started from Bicester itself or ran between Paddington and Birmingham. The slip coach from the 5.10pm fast to Wolverhampton also became part of a stopping train when it was attached at Bicester to the 6.34pm all-stations to Banbury. Gradually the stopping service on this route was curtailed. Blackthorn station was closed in 1953, Brill & Ludgershall became an unstaffed halt in 1956. With the exception of Bicester and Kings Sutton, the remaining stations were closed on 7 January 1963, when all intermediate services were withdrawn.

To complete the chapter on services we come to what is probably the most interesting part of the route. From Princes Risborough southwards we are now on the Great Central/Great Western joint line and passenger train working on this section has throughout the years reflected the joint ownership of the line.

Although an extensive suburban service was run from Marylebone to High Wycombe, we must not forget that the GC regularly used the route for many of its express services to and from the North. Trains to such destinations as Sheffield, Manchester and Bradford were regular daily visitors on the route; the latter at one time even slipped a coach at Grendon Underwood on its route to the North. This use of the joint line continued throughout LNER days and well into the BR years. However, the 1950s saw many of these services return to the ex-GC route via Aylesbury. One surprise however was when in 1956 the Eastern Region switched the evening 'Master Cutler' express to Sheffield

Top left:
2-6-2T No 3101 pauses at Henley-in-Arden on an April day in 1957, with a Snow Hill-Stratford-upon-Avon stopping service. Real Photos (K3365)

Above left:
Non-auto-fitted 0-4-2T No 5813 stands at Bearley with the local stopping service from Leamington to Stratford-upon-Avon in May 1957.
Real Photos (K3427)

Left:
Recent reballasting work is in evidence as 2-6-2T No 5104 pauses at Grimes Hill with a service from Moor Street to Henley-in-Arden in May 1957.
Real Photos (K3423)

back on to the joint route. This was to be short-lived however, for with the transfer of the joint line to London Midland Region control in 1958, the 'Master Cutler' service was transferred to King's Cross. The only regular service to continue to use the route was the 12.15pm Marylebone-Manchester, which called at High Wycombe to pick up on its journey northwards. By the 1960s regular through passenger working on the joint line had all but ceased with just the occasional special using the route via Grendon Underwood.

Whilst the ex-GC main line services were rather spasmodic, that could not be said of the suburban services. From the earliest days of the joint line an extensive intermediate service between Marylebone and High Wycombe had been run by the Great Central. It must be remembered that at this time areas such as South Ruislip, Denham, Gerrards Cross and Beaconsfield were but small villages. The opening of the railway brought for many the added opportunity to live in the quiet Middlesex and Buckinghamshire countryside and commute to London. Unfortunately it brought with it the outward spread of the population, eventually making some of these desirable areas into just one more suburb of London.

To accommodate the many commuters an hourly weekday service was the order of the day, being strengthened at peak times to give what amounted to a half-hourly service. This intensity of working continued right up until the end of steam traction. During the 1950s and early 1960s there were some 26 trains per day each way between High Wycombe and Marylebone. During peak times, some of these ran right through to Princes Risborough and Haddenham; other services ran through to Aylesbury. Even on Sundays an hourly service was provided on the line, with two of the trains running via Ashen-

don Junction through to Brackley. These served all of the intermediate stations south of High Wycombe. The only major change that took place was one of motive power; whereas before 1958 Eastern Region motive power had been the rule of the day, the transfer of the joint line to London Midland Region control during that year resulted in an almost immediate switch-over to ex-LMS locomotive types. In June 1962 steam traction was withdrawn from suburban services on the Chiltern lines, with the service being completely dieselised using new Derby four-car DMU sets.

In anticipation of this the platforms at Beaconsfield, Gerrards Cross and Denham had been lengthened during 1961.

With such an excellent suburban service being operated to and from Marylebone we must not forget that the GWR and latterly the Western Region also operated their own local services on the route. Princes Risborough-Aylesbury was operated on the auto-train principle, with usually an ex-GWR '1400' or '5400' auto-fitted locomotive and one coach providing up to eight trips per day in each direction; this was supplemented by the addition of some through trains to and from Maidenhead and Slough. Some services from Oxford via the

Above:
0-4-2T No 1453 together with auto-coach *Thrush* are seen here at Aynho troughs with the 11.05am stopping service from Banbury to Princes Risborough on 19 May 1962. A. Vickers

Left:
Ex-GW 0-6-0PT No 4650 at the small terminus station at Watlington, shortly after arriving with the 12.40pm Saturdays-only service from Princes Risborough on 29 July 1956.
G. F. Bannister

Thame branch were generally only advertised to the public as far as Princes Risborough, but did in fact work through to High Wycombe and Paddington via Bourne End. The Watlington branch, which was closed to passengers in 1957, had provided a service of five trains each way on weekdays. An interesting feature of this service for a number of years was the attachment of one of the slip coaches from the 7.10pm ex-Paddington on to the 8.00pm departure to Watlington. GW services south of High Wycombe ran via Bourne End and Maidenhead, on the original Wycombe Railway route. Between Maidenhead and High Wycombe there were some 12 trains a day in either direction, some of these at peak hours running through to both Slough and Paddington.

We must not forget the services that had been provided at the London end for many years. The stretch of track between Old Oak Common and Northolt at one time contained no

fewer than nine halts. Services were operated on this line in the early years by GW steam railmotors. Eventually the railmotors were withdrawn and very soon after the halts at North Acton and Twyford Abbey were closed, but the line continued to be worked by GW autotrains. In 1935 London Transport decided to extend its Central Line from North Acton to Ruislip. The new line was built parallel to the old GWR line, with new LT stations

replacing the old halts. Delayed by World War 2, the new electrified route was eventually opened as far as Greenford on 30 June 1947 and to West Ruislip on 19 November 1948. After this date the GW local service was withdrawn, leaving just the Greenford-Ealing shuttle service intact. By the mid-1950s this was being operated by ex-GW diesel rail-cars, which were eventually replaced by single-car DMUs.

Above:
The unusual sight of ex-LNER 'L1' 2-6-4T No 67800 from King's Cross shed piloting ex-GWR 0-6-0PT No 7763 on the Aylesbury branch auto-train at Princes Risborough on 13 August 1955.
S. Creer

Right:
Banbury-based 5400 class 0-6-0PT No 5424 leaves High Wycombe with the stopping service to Banbury on 6 June 1953. Brian Morrison

3
Freight Services

Prior to the opening of the cut-off route, GWR goods and parcels traffic from London to the Midlands was required to travel along the heavily congested lines via Oxford. The freedom from this congestion and shorter route mileage that the new line allowed was soon exploited by the GWR with the introduction of express vacuum-fitted goods trains running between Paddington, Wolverhampton and Birkenhead. Some of these services were to remain almost unchanged for nearly 50 years. Many of these trains carried perishables such as fruit and meat; in fact the evening meat train from Birkenhead to Paddington was a feature of the line for over 40 years. Another overnight vacuum-fitted perishable was the 12.10am from Park Royal to Oxley Sidings which had a regular loading of some 64 wagons. Coal was an important commodity that was carried in large amounts, with many trains running daily over the route. Some,

Below:
Ex-LMS Stanier Class 5 No 45393 is seen here passing the small yard at Beaconsfield with an up parcels train to Marylebone on a sunny day in 1957.
J. D. Edwards

such as the daily service from Leamington to Old Oak, had loadings of more than 70 wagons. Services ran between the yards at Paddington and Acton to Banbury, Bordesley and Oxley, carrying milk, fish and other perishables.

To improve freight services generally, the Great Western carried out a series of improvements to the various yards on the route as follows:

1907 New yard and locomotive depot at Oxley, Wolverhampton
1918 Remodelled and enlarged yard at Bordesley Junction, Birmingham
1931 New 2,000 wagon hump yard opened at Banbury
1942 Extra sidings installed at Banbury Junction.

In the period after the war some 28 goods and parcels trains were using the new line south of Banbury daily. Some of these, such as the 8.05pm Dorrington (Shrewsbury)-Marylebone milk train, travelled on the route all the way from Wolverhampton before using the junction at Northolt to arrive at Marylebone at 1.10am. Other interesting night-time workings were the 1.10am Marylebone-Crewe parcels and the 7.35pm Marylebone-Shrewsbury milk empties, both of these using ER motive power as far as Banbury.

The joint section from Ashendon to Northolt was extensively used by goods and parcels services running to and from the ex-Great Central line. A considerable number of goods trains ran nightly between the large yards at Woodford Halse to and from the yards at Slough, North Acton and Neasden. Much of this was coal traffic from the Nottingham pits. Other long-distance services via Ashendon Junction were the 3.15pm Newcastle-Acton and the 8.35pm Marylebone-York parcels. In the 1950s and early 1960s up to 12 goods and parcels trains were running each way daily on to the ex-GC main line by way of Ashendon Junction. Two of these, the Marylebone-Nottingham newspaper train and the Woodford Halse-Neasden house coal service were still operated by steam traction well into 1965. Another interesting working which ran for many years was the twice weekly Class C Guinness train from the Park Royal brewery to Newcastle.

Pick-up services on the joint line and cut-off route were provided by Banbury-Acton and Woodford-High Wycombe services and engines from these pick-up goods trains would be used to shunt the various small yards en route. Stations and yards at the northern end of the cut-off route were served by the 6.45am Banbury Junction-Brill goods which returned to Banbury Junction at 10.25am. Other goods services joined the line at

Below:
'2251' class 0-6-0 No 2290 crosses the 181yd viaduct over the Grand Union Canal to the south of Denham with an up pick-up goods on 11 April 1953. Denham West Junction signalbox can be seen to the left. Brian Morrison

Right:
Bourne End was the main intermediate station on the Wycombe Railway branch from Maidenhead to High Wycombe. On 7 July 1962, 2-6-2T No 6128 enters Bourne End with a mixed goods from High Wycombe. L. Sandler

Below right:
An unidentified WD 2-8-0 makes a spectacular sight as it climbs Saunderton Bank with a trainload of coal empties. Mike Pope

Left:

A rather motley collection of empty coal wagons is hauled through Leamington Spa by '5600' 0-6-2T No 6657 on 25 August 1952. The ex-LNWR station at Leamington Avenue can just be seen behind the locomotive. Brian Morrison

Below left:

Ex-LMS 'Royal Scot' No 46106 *Gordon Highlander* takes water at Lapworth troughs on its journey from Washwood Heath to Hinksey Yard, with a part-fitted freight on 20 September 1961. M. Mensing

Bottom left:

Ex-LMS 'Crab' 2-6-0 No 42827 passes through Lapworth with the 4.40pm Hinksey-Water Orton freight on 9 July 1958. T. E. Williams

Above right:

Ex-WD 2-8-0 No 90630 passes Bentley Heath crossing with a down empty freight on Sunday 3 July 1960. Behind the locomotive can be seen the sidings which served the World War 2 Ministry of Food cold store. M. Mensing

Right:

Standard '9F' 2-10-0 No 92120 storms through Knowle & Dorridge station with a down freight from Hinksey yard, Oxford, to Washwood Heath on 14 August 1959. M. Mensing

Below right:

Some rather mediocre work for a pair of express passenger 4-6-0s as No 7019 *Fowey Castle* restarts the 12.50pm Birmingham Snow Hill-Leamington and catches ex-LMS 'Royal Scot' 4-6-0 No 46118 *Royal Welsh Fusilier* on an up freight at Acocks Green & South Yardley on 27 January 1962. M. Mensing

Risborough. From the Thame branch, the 3.30pm Worcester-Acton mixed freight travelled via Oxford and Thame, as did the 11.05am Hinksey-Slough via Bourne End. The 9.40pm Aylesbury-Paddington mixed goods was one of the few goods services to traverse the Aylesbury-Risborough branch, running into London via Bourne End and Maidenhead.

As can be seen, the cut-off route and joint line were used to great advantage by both the GW and the Great Central to provide fast easy access from London to the Midlands; a tradition that continued well into the final days of steam traction on the line.

At Aynho Junction freight services from the cut-off route had to compete for track space with the vast amount of goods, parcels and coal traffic running to and from the south via Oxford. Much of the traffic originated in the large yards at Banbury, Bordesley and Oxley. Banbury in particular was the starting point for many goods workings. In the early 1960s the limestone quarry at Bishops Itchington (Greaves cement works) was

Left:
BR Standard '9F' 2-10-0 No 92208 is seen approaching Tyseley with a mixed freight from the London area.
P. J. Sharpe

Below:
Ex-GW 0-6-0PT No 8700 is seen here shunting in the up yard at Tyseley on 30 August 1958. The engine still carries a GWR roundel on its tanks some 10 years after Nationalisation.
M. Mensing

Bottom:
0-6-0PT No 9798 is seen here passing Moor Street on its approach to Snow Hill Tunnel, with a down goods on 27 February 1960. M. Mensing

almost worked out. In order to continue cement production, limestone was carried from Ardley quarry (south of Banbury) by a special limestone train that ran daily. Coal for the cement works was carried on the local pick-up service from either Banbury or Leamington.

The line from Woodford via Banbury Junction brought many goods services on to the route. Several of these continued southwards to Oxford and beyond; others were remarshalled in the yards at Banbury. Working time-tables show over 20 coal, parcels and general goods trains arriving and departing daily via this route. As already mentioned, the yards at Banbury were extensively enlarged in 1931 and again in 1942 making them one of the busiest on the whole of the Western Region. At the height of its operations, some 42 goods trains daily were originating or terminating at Banbury yards. Iron ore in particular

Top:
'5600' class 0-6-2T No 6674 emerges from under the train shed roof at Snow Hill with a down freight on 15 February 1958. M. Mensing

Above left:
An up parcels service is seen near West Bromwich in the capable hands of No 6937 *Conyngham Hall* on 20 September 1958. M. Mensing

Left:
2-6-2T No 3102 is seen shunting in Stafford Road yard prior to leaving with a freight for Wrexham on 17 July 1954. Brian Morrison

was moved in great amounts from the many quarries in the area and formed an important part of the goods services for over half a century. For many years between seven and 10 trains were leaving the ironstone sidings at Banbury, supplying ore to the furnaces of the West Midlands and South Wales. At this point it is worth describing the biggest producer in the area: Oxfordshire Ironstone Co.

The Oxfordshire Ironstone Railway

Apart from coal, iron ore was probably the second most important mineral in this country, with the annual tonnage extracted being surpassed worldwide only by the United States. There is certainly evidence that iron ore has been mined in this country since 200BC. One large ore area lies to the north of the county of Oxford and is known as the Oxfordshire Field. Although ore has been quarried in this field for many years, it was only during the latter half of the 19th century that use was made of local railway systems to aid transport of the ore.

Probably the best known company operating in the Oxfordshire Field was the suitably named Oxfordshire Ironstone Co. Formed in 1917, the share capital was provided by three of the country's major iron and steel manufacturers: Stewarts & Lloyds, Baldwins Ltd, and the Brymbo Steel Co. With many of the other smaller ironstone companies operating in the area choosing to use narrow gauge rail systems, the Oxford Ironstone Co built a standard gauge line that was not only fully signalled but operated upwards of 20 locomotives over its 10 miles of track.

This large system was opened in 1919 and ran from exchange sidings alongside the Great Western main line approximately 1¼ miles north of Banbury station to quarry sites at Wroxton and Hornton some five miles away. Originally built as a single-track line, by 1953 the system had been doubled throughout. A small workshop and engine shed were situated at the Banbury end at Pinhill Farm which was approximately one mile from the exchange sidings with the GW main line. From here the line continued to Wroxton, a distance of about two miles. The company's headquarters were situated here, together with another engine shed, extensive sidings and a large stone crusher. On this section the line also crossed two roads, where gated level crossings were provided together with controlling signalboxes and signals. These items, together with the gradient posts and lineside telegraph, certainly gave this industrial line a 'main line' feel.

From Wroxton the line continued to several quarry sites eventually terminating at Hornton. During the 1950s the output of the quarry system was running at some two million tons per year, necessitating the use of up to 20 locomotives. For operating purposes the railway was effectively divided into two halves, the Wroxton-Hornton section was worked by the smaller 0-4-0 tank engines and the section from Wroxton to Banbury by the larger 0-6-0 tank locomotives. The rundown of the quarries took place during the 1960s as quarries were

Below:
Oxfordshire Ironstone Railway Hunslet 0-6-0ST *Spencer*, built 1941, is seen here approaching Wroxton on 25 March 1965, with a load of empty ironstone wagons. This section of the ironstone railway was doubled in 1953.
Mike Soden

Right:
The sad sight of eight withdrawn ironstone railway locomotives at Wroxton on 25 March 1965. By this date many of the remaining services on the ironstone railway had been dieselised.
Mike Soden

Below right:
Iron ore for the industrial Midlands hauled by 2-6-0 No 5390 passes Hatton North Junction with a Banbury-Bilston ironstone train on 9 April 1955.
T. E. Williams

worked out and planning permission was not forthcoming to open up new reserves. Towards the end, steam traction was only used spasmodically, most of the traffic having passed into the hands of several new 0-4-0 diesel locomotives purchased during 1964/65. The end came on 30 September 1967 when production of ore ceased.

The ore was distributed by special ironstone trains which ran from the Ironstone Sidings on the Western Region main line. During 1954 these were as follows:

10.55am Oxford Ironstone Sidings-Cardiff
11.30am Oxford Ironstone Sidings-Bilston West (Stewarts & Lloyds)
12.55pm Oxford Ironstone Sidings-Bilston West (Stewarts & Lloyds)
 1.30pm Oxford Ironstone Sidings-Margam
 4.45pm Oxford Ironstone Sidings-Bilston West (Stewarts & Lloyds)
 6.50pm Oxford Ironstone Sidings-Cardiff and Margam
 9.10pm Oxford Ironstone Sidings-Bilston West (Stewarts & Lloyds).

Many of the South Wales services to and from Banbury travelled via Hatton, Stratford-upon-Avon and Honeybourne. Hatton South Junction was used by up to 12 goods trains per day. The majority of these were iron ore, coal and general goods services from Banbury to Severn Tunnel Junction and Cardiff, but there were also two local pick-up goods, the 6.15am Leamington-Stratford-upon-Avon and the evening 7.45pm Leamington-Honeybourne. Many goods services joined the route at Leamington via the ex-LNWR Coventry branch. Many of these were coal trains from various Midland collieries that terminated at either Leamington or Banbury yards.

The North Warwicks line from Tyseley provided an excellent through route and was extensively used by various goods services. From the earliest days of its opening there was upwards of a dozen or so through workings, some lasting well into post-Nationalisation days. By the late 1950s there were 16 booked workings each way daily, with many long-distance hauls from the yards at Bordesley and Oxley, to destinations such as Marazion, Tavistock, Newton Abbot and Westbury. Local services on the line were provided by the 10.35am Bordesley-Henley-in-Arden pick-up goods; the locomotive on this train shunting the small yards en route. Quite a number of services ran to and from Honeybourne, where they were either remarshalled or continued via the OW&WR route to their destinations. Two such workings to do this were the 8.00pm Lye-Moreton Cutting and the 2.15am Oxley-Basingstoke. In 1964 over 60,000 tons of goods per

Top:
A very clean Mogul No 6394 runs off the Stratford line at Hatton station with a return train of ironstone empties from Cardiff to Banbury on 29 September 1962. M. Pope

Above right:
A busy moment at Leamington on 25 August 1952 with 2-8-2T No 7243 running through on a down iron ore train, passing Standard 2-6-2T No 82002 on a Leamington-Worcester service. An unidentified 0-6-0PT can also be seen shunting in the adjacent Leamington Avenue yard.
Brian Morrison

Right:
During the 1960s, limestone was shipped from Ardley quarry to Greaves cement works at Harbury. On 29 August 1962, '5100' class 2-6-2T No 4176 hauls a limestone train away from the cut-off route, at Aynho Junction. M. Mensing

week was passing over the North Warwicks route.

Bordesley is probably the oldest yard on the route, being opened as early as 1852. At one time the main engine shed for the Birmingham area was situated here. This was removed in 1908 and the yard was subsequently enlarged. Bordesley has always been busy with interchange traffic between here and the nearby Midland yards at Washwood Heath and Water Orton. A considerable number of goods services to and from Bordesley ran via the North Warwicks line to destinations such as Honeybourne, Stoke Gifford, Swindon and Bristol. Other services ran to and from Paddington and Acton yards.

Above:
Standard '4MT' 2-6-4T No 80072 takes water alongside Banbury MPD, whilst en route from Ardley Quarry to Greaves Sidings with a trainload of limestone on 22 May 1965. Mike Soden

Left:
'5300' class 2-6-0 No 5332 on a down freight, passes through the attractive surroundings of Shirley station on 29 August 1959. M. Mensing

Oxley Sidings was the smallest of these three main yards, but was of equal importance. It was situated a couple of miles north of Wolverhampton Low Level station on the line to Shrewsbury. A large proportion of goods services leaving the yard travelled southwards along the route. Many incoming services ran into the yard from Shrewsbury and North Wales before being resorted and despatched southwards. In the 1950s, for instance, there were six daily goods services to and from yards at Paddington, Acton and Southall and several

Far left:
2-8-0 No 3851 puts up quite a smoke screen as it approaches Spring Road station on the North Warwicks line with a down freight on 29 September 1960. M. Mensing

Below far left:
The Stratford-upon-Avon-Leamington local coal empties leave Hatton behind 2-6-2T No 4178 on 17 March 1956. T. E. Williams

Left:
The small station at Chinnor is still largely intact a couple of years after closure to passengers. Hawksworth 0-6-0PT No 1636 is seen arriving from Princes Risborough to shunt the small yard here. J. D. Edwards

Below left:
2-6-2T No 6117 tops Saunderton Summit with an up goods service from Aylesbury in July 1961. C. R. L. Coles

Below:
No 6905 *Claughton Hall* makes a fine sight as it heads a northbound freight through the Buckinghamshire countryside near Beaconsfield on 19 December 1963. Gerald T. Robinson

daily mixed goods services to the southwest. Some of these, such as the 9.00pm to Newton Abbot, the 9.15pm to Tavistock and the 9.45pm to Westbury travelled during the hours of darkness. These latter three services ran via Stratford-upon-Avon and Cheltenham. It is impossible within the scope of this book to give any more than a brief insight of goods services on the route, but I hope that I have conveyed the feeling of both the diversity and intensity of goods services over this most interesting of routes.

4
The Final Years

In the early 1960s, with the electrification on the Euston route in full swing, the cut-off route was enjoying its busiest period ever. Apart from the hourly interval service, many additional relief trains were incorporated into the timetables, especially at weekends. By the end of 1962 all of the main line services on the direct route between Paddington and Wolverhampton had been dieselised and were attracting growing numbers of passengers. It really seemed inconceivable that within a few short years through goods and passenger services over the cut-off route would, to all intents and purposes, cease to exist.

DMUs had started to replace steam traction on the Birmingham area suburban services as early as 1957, when they were introduced on to the Leamington and North Warwicks line. By the end of the decade steam traction had become the exception rather than the rule on many lines. The public obviously favoured the new diesel trains, for local passenger journeys in the Birmingham area had risen by over one million in 1959 alone. At the south end of the route DMUs were rapidly replacing steam traction on the Chiltern line suburban services to and from Marylebone, and from June 1962 they had ousted steam completely, Neasden shed being closed during the same month.

The withdrawal of the 'Kings' from the route on 10 September 1962 saw all direct line express services south of Wolverhampton become diesel-hauled, and for a few short months the direct route took on the air of a modern

Below:

The new and the old meet as No 6007 *King William III* passes a new Type 4 'Western' diesel-hydraulic at Ranelagh Bridge yard. The 'King' is on the 4.10pm service to Wolverhampton and still at this date (4 September 1962) looks in fine external condition. The 'Kings' were replaced by the 'Westerns' from 10 September 1962. No 6007 was officially withdrawn just four days after this picture was taken. J. Carter

Above:
A summer Saturday holiday service hauled by No 5026 *Criccieth Castle* climbs Hatton Bank on 22 August 1964. Mike Pope

Right:
Ex-WD 2-8-0 No 90365 runs off the Oxford line at Aynho Junction with a long train load of empty coal wagons on 29 August 1962. M. Mensing

Below right:
The last two regular steam turns from Stratford-upon-Avon are seen here on 3 March 1963. No 6817 *Gwenddwr Grange* heads the 8.30am to Snow Hill, with 0-6-0 No 2211 on the 8.43am service to Leamington. G. England

successful railway. This was to be short-lived, for on 7 January 1963 all intermediate stations on the cut-off route between Banbury and Princes Risborough, with the exception of Bicester, were closed. On the same date passenger services between Oxford and Princes Risborough were also withdrawn.

On 15 August 1963 one of the new 'Western' class diesel-hydraulics, No D1040 *Western Queen*, standing in on the 'Birmingham Pullman' due to failure of the 'Blue Pullman' unit, collided with a freight train at Knowle & Dorridge, with unfortunately the driver of the 'Western' suffering fatal injuries.

In September 1963, Western Region lines from Aynho Junction northwards passed into the control of the

London Midland Region. At this time Snow Hill was still a thriving station with some 373 passenger trains calling daily, carrying between 9,000 and 10,000 passengers. Over 100 goods trains were still passing through the station every 24hr, many still at this time steam-hauled.

The LMR soon decided to phase out steam traction altogether, particularly on the remaining steam-hauled passenger services. Stafford Road was closed in September 1963 and its remaining engines were transferred to Oxley. The last two regular steam-powered passenger services on the North Warwicks line, the 8.30am from Stratford to Moor Street and the 8.43am to Leamington were dieselised during the autumn of 1964. The last

Top:
A return football excursion from Birmingham to Southampton approaches Solihull behind rebuilt 'West Country' 4-6-2 No 34028 *Eddystone* **on 27 April 1963. This was one of several such specials run in connection with this FA Cup game.** M. Mensing

Above left:
One of the few remaining steam suburban trains from Snow Hill was the 5.37pm service to Dudley, seen here in the down bay platform at Snow Hill on 19 May 1964 in the hands of 2-6-2T No 4155. G. Greenslade

Left:
'Castle' No 5056 *Earl of Powis* **runs past Hatton South Junction with an up parcels train in July 1964. Note the rows of redundant guards' vans in the sidings.** Real Photos (K6676)

steam-hauled rush-hour service ran from Snow Hill to Worcester on 4 September 1964.

The sole remaining steam-hauled passenger service continued to run between Snow Hill and Leamington right up until 31 December 1965. Steam traction was still being used extensively on goods services over much of the route, but these services also became diesel-powered as one by one the steam sheds were closed, and by the end of 1966 steam had been completely eliminated from lines south of Wolverhampton. The last regular steam-hauled passenger train over the cut-off route, the 4.15pm intermediate service from Paddington to Banbury, was steam-hauled for the last time on 11 June 1965.

The rundown of the North Warwicks line as a through route started

Right:
No 6967 *Willesley Hall* minus nameplates rescues a failed DMU at Solihull on 18 May 1965. Note the recently removed yard here.
M. Mensing

Below right:
'4100' class 2-6-2T No 4147 at Budbrooke with the 8.45am Sundays-only Leamington-Birkenhead service on 29 August 1965. J. R. P. Hunt

Bottom:
No 7022 *Hereford Castle* devoid of name and numberplates stands at Bicester North with the 4.15pm semi-fast from Paddington to Banbury on 13 April 1965. This was the last regular steam-hauled passenger turn over the joint section.
Derek Tuck

in September 1962 when passenger services from Birmingham to South Wales were diverted away from the North Warwicks line on to the Lickey route. A twice-daily passenger service between Stratford and Gloucester continued until March 1968, after which all passenger services south of Stratford-upon-Avon were withdrawn. Through goods services had succumbed a year earlier on 6 March 1967 when the remaining few services were withdrawn. This had hardly seemed likely in 1962, when from 13 June much of the general goods and iron ore traffic from Woodford Halse and Banbury to South Wales was re-routed via a new connection at

Fenny Compton on to the old SMJ line to Stratford. By March 1965, however, traffic had dwindled to such an extent that a few remaining services which had by now been dieselised, were re-routed to run either via Didcot or the Lickey route.

Once the electrification work on the Euston line was completed, many of the main line passenger services to Wolverhampton were switched back to the Euston route. From 6 March 1967 all main line passenger services were withdrawn from Snow Hill. The last through service from Paddington to Wolverhampton and Birkenhead ran on 4 March, hauled for part of the way by the privately-owned No 7029 *Clun Castle*. The few services that remained on the cut-off route now ran from Paddington to New Street via Bordesley Junction. Within a few years all but one of these remaining services were switched to the Oxford line.

The withdrawal of through services meant that Snow Hill, that proudest of stations, was now left only with a few local DMU services. On 2 March 1968 another nail was driven into its coffin when services southwards from Snow Hill were diverted into either Moor Street or New Street stations and the tunnel was closed. This now left the single-car DMU shuttle service to Wolverhampton and Langley Green. Through goods traffic had been diverted away from Snow Hill a few months previously. During 1969 Snow Hill became unstaffed; at one time over 350 people were employed here. It now became arguably the largest unstaffed halt in the country. In this same year the old GWR hotel was demolished.

The saddest blow of all came during 1972 with the closure of Snow Hill, and the route to Wolverhampton. The end came on 6 March, when the remaining service between Snow Hill and Wolverhampton Low Level was withdrawn and all intermediate stations were closed. Thus in five short years a once-busy through route, together with one of the finest stations on the Western Region, had passed into history.

Above:
No 7029 *Clun Castle* (minus nameplates) leaves Greaves Sidings near Harbury in July 1966 with coal empties for Banbury yard. The 'Castle' was at this time privately owned.
J. R. P. Hunt

Left:
The last days of steam at Banbury, where Standard Class 5 No 73117 takes water after its arrival from Bournemouth, whilst Brush Type 4 No D1869 prepares to take the service onwards to Newcastle on 18 June 1966.
Mike Soden

Once the cut-off route was opened and the GWR was able to introduce 2hr express workings between Paddington and Birmingham, motive power was provided by examples of the two-cylinder 'Saints' and the four-cylinder 'Stars'. These 4-6-0 engines soon dominated the express workings on the new route, Wolverhampton Stafford Road having an allocation of 19 of these types: 11 'Saints' and eight 'Stars'. Occasionally other types could be seen, with the 4-4-0 'Bulldog' and 'County' classes making the odd appearance, although these engines were really too small to maintain the schedules. Goods traffic on the line was mostly in the hands of examples of the 'Aberdare' and '4300' class 2-6-0s and the older 'Dean Goods' and 'Beyer' class 0-6-0s.

The period between the wars saw a considerable change in motive power on the line. The 'Stars' and 'Saints' that had performed so admirably were gradually replaced by the new 'King' and 'Castle' class locomotives. The first 'Kings' appeared on the route during 1928 when Nos 6017 and 6019 were allocated to Stafford Road. 'Castles' made their first appearances just one

year later. The introduction of these engines gave quite a power advantage over the older counterparts. For whereas on the express working the maximum load for a 'Star' was set at 320 tons, the 'Castles' upped this to 355 tons and the 'Kings' to a massive 400 tons. By the mid-1930s Stafford Road's allocation contained four 'Saints', five 'Stars', five 'Castles' and five 'Kings'.

The newly introduced 'Hall' and 'Grange' class 4-6-0s started to appear on the route in the period prior to World War 2, and were used mainly on intermediate passenger services. Goods traffic also saw some change in motive power with '2800' class 2-8-0s and newer '4300' 2-6-0s ousting many of the older locomotive types. Some of the overnight fitted goods and parcel trains were operated for many years by examples of Churchward's massive '4700' class 2-8-0. It is interesting to note that Oxley shed during this period had an allocation of some 30 '4300' class 2-6-0s and six 'Hall' class 4-6-0s, used mainly for goods traffic duties.

GW local services at both ends of the line had been operated over the years

by various examples of 2-6-2T types. Up until the mid-1930s suburban traffic in the outer Birmingham area was in the hands of '3150' class and '3900' class 2-6-2T, supplemented by the '3600' class 2-4-2T. Traffic at the London end was dominated by the '3100' class 2-6-2T. Gradually, however, as newer types of locomotives were introduced, the older classes were withdrawn from the services. By the start of World War 2 these older locomotives had all but disappeared, leaving local services at both ends of the line in the hands of the newer 2-6-2Ts, with Wolverhampton-Birmingham and the Leamington-Birmingham-North Warwicks services operated by '4100', '5100' and '8100' class 2-6-2Ts based at Stafford Road, Tyseley and Leamington. At the London end, the Maidenhead-Princes

Below:
'4300' class Mogul No 6351 runs through the cutting at Harbury with an up horse box special in April 1960.
T. E. Williams

Right:
No 5991 *Gresham Hall* passes the small coal yard at Warwick with a down ironstone train from Banbury on 8 May 1958. M. Mensing

Below right:
The 7.45pm Leamington-Stratford stopping service leaves Warwick station on 8 May 1958 hauled by 'Large Prairie' No 4118. Fellow member of the class No 4128 can be seen standing in the down bay on banking duties.
M. Mensing

Bottom:
No 1022 *County of Northampton* climbs Hatton Bank with a through train from Bournemouth to Birkenhead (via Oxford) on 12 January 1957.
T. E. Williams

Risborough-Aylesbury services were almost exclusively operated by '6100' class 2-6-2Ts supplied by Old Oak and Slough depots. A change of motive power also took place on the two major branch line services along the route. Watlington and Aylesbury were for many years operated by examples of the '517' class 0-4-2T engines, but after the mid-1930s by either auto-fitted '1400' 0-4-2T or '5400' or '6400' 0-6-0PTs.

In this form the services were operated on the line until the end of steam traction. A notable landmark was the withdrawal of the last 'Star' from the route during 1957, the locomotive being No 4061 *Glastonbury Abbey* of Stafford Road depot.

In 1959 the Stafford Road allocation stood at eight 'Kings' and 14 'Castles'. However, the biggest impact on the

Right:
Possibly one of the last steam-hauled passenger services to traverse the Watlington branch was the LCGB's 'Six Counties' rail tour, seen here leaving Princes Risborough on 3 April 1960 hauled by 0-4-2T No 1473. S. Creer

Below:
Stafford Road's last 'Star' No 4061 *Glastonbury Abbey* is seen entering Snow Hill on 4 August 1956 with a holiday relief train. The engine lasted for just one more year. M. Mensing

Below:
The rare sight of ex-LMS 'Patriot' No 45504 *Royal Signals* about to leave Snow Hill with the 6.00pm stopping service to Wolverhampton on 24 February 1962. Notice also the coach identification signs installed for the 'Birmingham Pullman' service suspended from the roof above the locomotive. M. Mensing

route since its opening was the introduction during 1960 of the one-hour interval services which lasted for the duration of the electrification of the Euston-Wolverhampton route. To facilitiate this, 27 of the 'Kings' were allocated to the route, 11 at Stafford Road and 16 at Old Oak Common. This was but a swan song for these excellent locomotives, for in September 1962 they were withdrawn from the route *en bloc*. Three 'Kings' in particular deserve mention for their longevity at one depot. Nos 6005 *King George II*, 6006 *King George I* and 6008 *King James II* were each allocated to Stafford Road for over 30 years.

Left:
Ex-LNER Class A5 4-6-2T No 69814 hardly disturbs the tranquility of the Chiltern countryside near High Wycombe as it makes its way from Princes Risborough to Marylebone on 6 June 1953. Brian Morrison

Bottom:
Ex-LNER 'V2' 2-6-2 No 60878 (38C) passes High Wycombe north yard with the 12.10pm Marylebone-Manchester c1957. This was one of the few ex-GC services still using the joint line at this time. J. D. Edwards

In June 1962 four new Type 4 'Western' class diesels, Nos D1000/2/4/5 were allocated to Oxley especially for the Paddington-Wolverhampton services. These together with examples from Old Oak Common took over all express passenger services from the start of the winter timetable on 10 September 1962, on which date all remaining 'King' class engines were withdrawn from the route. That is not the end of the story, however, for unreliability of the new diesels saw a number of instances of 'Kings' being reinstated to cover for failures. Two such examples occurred on 30 October 1962, when No 6011 *King James I* hauled the 10.00am Birmingham-Paddington and No 6000 *King George*

V itself appeared on the up 'Inter-City' as late as 3 November. Other ex-GW 4-6-0s continued the tradition, with examples of 'Castles', 'Granges' and 'Halls' making regular appearances well into 1965 on the semi-fast services. Closure of Stafford Road in 1963 saw much of its remaining steam allocation pass to nearby Oxley shed, including eight 'Castles', which continued to provide motive power for services northwards to Shrewsbury and Birkenhead, and also southwards either on the North Warwicks line or via the cut-off route to London.

Steam disappeared from passenger services on the cut-off route from 11 June 1965, when the last regular steam working, the 4.15pm inter-

mediate service from Paddington to Banbury was hauled by No 7029 *Clun Castle*. This, incidentally, was also the very last scheduled steam working from Paddington.

Perhaps the most interesting section of the line, as far as variety of motive power is concerned, was the joint section between Northolt and Ashendon Junctions, for apart from the ex-GW engines already described, there were the many ex-GC and LNER types on the Eastern Region workings. Main line services during Great Central days produced many examples of Robinson-designed locomotives: 'C4' and 'C5' class 4-4-2s, 4-6-0 Classes 'B2', 'B3', 'B8' and the famous 'D10' and 'D11' 4-4-0 'Directors'. Suburban services from Marylebone to High Wycombe, Princes Risborough and

Right:
Ex-LNER Class A3 Pacific No 60111 *Enterprise* **is seen leaving High Wycombe with the 12.15pm Marylebone-Manchester. High Wycombe was its only stop on the joint line section.**
J. D. Edwards

Below right:
Unusual motive power for a down ironstone train from Banbury is provided by ex-LNER 'B1' No 61384, which is seen running through Harbury cutting on its way northwards on 21 September 1965. M. Mensing

Bottom right:
Ex-LMS Class 5 No 44753 with Caprotti valve gear heads a down empty stock train past the small coal yard and goods shed at Beaconsfield on 30 July 1960.
K. L. Cook

Brackley were generally in the hands of Robinson 4-4-2 tanks of Classes C13 and C14, being supplemented with the larger 'A5' 4-6-2 tanks introduced in 1911. Many of these classes continued to give stalwart service on the ex-GC passenger services on the joint line well after the advent of World War 2. By the 1950s, main line services were being handled by 'A3' class Pacifics, 'V2' class 2-6-2s and 'B1' class 4-6-0s, and for a short time in the early 1950s, 'Sandringham' class 'B17' 4-6-0s. The suburban services were operated almost entirely by the newer 'L1' class 2-6-4Ts.

A change of motive power took place during 1958 when regional boundary changes transferred the ex-GC suburban services to the London Midland Region. Neasden, the ex-GC depot for Marylebone, soon lost much of its Eastern Region locomotive stud, this being replaced by examples of Fowler, Fairburn and Stanier 2-6-4 tanks, supplemented by a large allocation of the newer BR Standard 2-6-4 tanks. These engines now took over almost all of the suburban services. Regular double-headed workings were on the 4.00am Marylebone-High Wycombe parcels and the 5.10am Neasden-High Wycombe ECS. These brought motive power into Wycombe for four of the early morning up commuter trains, the 5.55am, 6.25am, 6.48am and 7.15am.

Main line workings continued to produce 'V2' and 'B1' classes but gradually these types were replaced with Stanier Class 5 and 'Royal Scot' 4-6-0s. The 'A3' Pacifics had been allocated away from the line during 1957. Neasden shed closed in 1962, by which time all of the Marylebone suburban services on the joint line had been dieselised. By this date only a couple of through trains a week were using the joint section. A brief mention must be made of Eastern Region freight workings on the joint line.

Left:
Fairburn 2-6-4T No 42251 is seen here at Banbury General as it waits to leave with the last local service between here and Woodford Halse on 13 June 1964. Mike Soden

Below:
Ex-WD 2-8-0 No 90207 clanks its way through Beaconsfield with some down coal empties. Beaconsfield, as with other stations on this part of the joint route, stands in a deep chalk cutting. J. D. Edwards

Bottom:
Standing outside Old Oak Common on 5 May 1956 are 'Castle' No 5065 *Newport Castle* **together with 'Hall' No 5941** *Campion Hall*. Brian Morrison

These could produce many different types of ex-GC and LNER engines, many of which have already been mentioned in regard to passenger haulage, but stalwarts on the line were the Gresley 'K3' class 2-6-0 and the Robinson 'O4' class 2-8-0, and in later years Austerity ex-WD 2-8-0, Stanier Class 5 and Standard '9F' 2-10-0. A regular evening working that took an Eastern locomotive along the cut-off line as far as Banbury was the 6.35pm Marylebone-Shrewsbury milk empties. This was usually hauled by either a 'B1' or a 'V2'.

The following pages show the allocation of steam locomotives at the six locomotive sheds situated between Paddington and Wolverhampton. For the purpose of completeness, I have included Old Oak Common and Oxley, as both of these provided a considerable amount of the motive power for the services on the route. The allocation lists are correct to 3 October 1959.

The table below charts the rapid decline of the steam locomotive on the route, totals as at August of each year.

Depot	1950	1960	1965
81A	193	164	Closed to steam
84A	66	48	Closed completely
84B	67	48	58
84C	70	43	23
84D	29	17	Closed completely
84E	118	56	29
Total	543	376	110

81A Old Oak Common

Old Oak Common was the largest engine shed on the Western Region. It was opened by the Great Western Railway on 17 March 1906 and replaced the old engine sheds at Westbourne Park that had been in use since 1852. Situated three miles west of Paddington, the new depot was arguably the most spectacular in the country. The main building measured some 444ft × 360ft and housed within its walls four 65ft turntables, each with 28 bays. These provided accommodation for some 112 tank and tender engines. To one side of the main building stood a 12-road locomotive repair shop.

In the yard, locomotive servicing facilities were provided in the form of a large double-sided coaling plant, over which the depot water supply was housed in a 290,000gal tank. Adjacent to the locomotive depot stood the main carriage sheds and sidings. Enlarged in the 1930s, the main carriage shed measured approximately 1,000ft in length and 450ft in width, and could accommodate some 400 carriages under its roof.

When opened, Old Oak, or Paddington as it was known at this time, had an allocation of 154 engines, by the 1930s this had risen to 187 and for many years the allocation hovered around this total. The late 1950s and early 1960s saw the steam allocation drop as dieselisation took hold. The shed was finally closed to steam traction on 22 March 1965. At the peak of its activity nearly 2,000 personnel were employed here.

Allocation

'1500' class	0-6-0PT	1500, 1503, 1504, 1505
'2251' class	0-6-0	2222, 2276, 2282
'4700' class	2-8-0	4700, 4701, 4702, 4704, 4708
'5700' class	0-6-0PT	3648, 3688, 3754, 4615, 4644, 5717, 5764, 7722, 7791, 8751, 8754, 8756, 8757, 8759, 8760, 8762, 8763, 8764, 8765, 8767, 8768, 8770, 8771, 8772, 8773, 9658, 9659, 9661, 9701, 9702, 9703, 9704, 9705, 9706, 9707, 9709, 9710, 9725, 9751, 9754, 9758, 9784
'6100' class	2-6-2T	6110, 6113, 6120, 6121, 6132, 6135, 6141, 6142, 6144, 6145, 6149, 6158, 6159, 6168
'9400' class	0-6-0PT	8459, 9400, 9405, 9410, 9411, 9412, 9414, 9416, 9418, 9419, 9420, 9423, 9469, 9479
Standard '9F'	2-10-0	92229, 92230, 92238, 92239, 92240, 92241, 92244, 92245, 92246, 92247
'King' class	4-6-0	6000 *King George V*; 6002 *King William IV*; 6003 *King George IV*; 6004 *King George III*; 6009 *King Charles II*; 6010 *King Charles I*; 6012 *King Edward VI*; 6015 *King Richard III*; 6018 *King Henry VI*; 6019 *King Henry V*; 6021 *King Richard II*; 6023 *King Edward II*; 6024 *King Edward I*; 6025 *King Henry III*; 6028 *King George VI*; 6029 *King Edward VIII*
'Hall' class	4-6-0	4919 *Donnington Hall*; 5923 *Colston Hall*; 5929 *Hanham Hall*; 5931 *Hatherley Hall*; 5932 *Haydon Hall*; 5939 *Tangley Hall*; 5954 *Faendre Hall*; 5958 *Knolton Hall*; 5976 *Ashwicke Hall*; 5987 *Brocket Hall*; 6920 *Barningham Hall*.
'Modified Hall' class	4-6-0	6959 *Peatling Hall*; 6961 *Steadham Hall*; 6962 *Stoughton Hall*; 6966 *Witchingham Hall*; 6974 *Bryngwyn Hall*; 6978 *Haroldstone Hall*; 6990 *Witherslack Hall*; 7902 *Eaton Mascot Hall*; 7903 *Foremarke Hall*; 7904 *Fountains Hall*; 7927 *Willington Hall*
'Castle' class	4-6-0	4082 *Windsor Castle*; 4096 *Highclere Castle*; 5008 *Raglan Castle*; 5014 *Goodrich Castle*; 5027 *Farleigh Castle*; 5034 *Corfe Castle*; 5035 *Coity Castle*; 5040 *Stokesay Castle*; 5043 *Earl of Mount Edgcumbe*; 5044 *Earl of Dunraven*; 5052 *Earl of Radnor*; 5056 *Earl of Powis*; 5060 *Earl of Berkeley*; 5065 *Newport Castle*; 5066 *Sir Felix Pole*; 5074 *Hampden*; 5080 *Defiant*; 5084 *Reading Abbey*; 5087 *Tintern Abbey*; 5093 *Upton Castle*; 7001 *Sir James Milne*; 7004 *Eastnor Castle*; 7010 *Avondale Castle*; 7013 *Bristol Castle*; 7017 *G. J. Churchward*; 7020 *Gloucester Castle*; 7024 *Powis Castle*; 7025 *Sudeley Castle*; 7027 *Thornbury Castle*; 7030 *Cranbrook Castle*; 7032 *Denbigh Castle*; 7033 *Hartlebury Castle*; 7036 *Taunton Castle*

Total: 164

Above:
Looking tired and rather forlorn, two 'Kings' Nos 6017 *King Edward IV* and 6013 *King Henry VIII* stand in the yard at Wolverhampton on 3 July 1962, just a few days away from withdrawal.
Richard McAvoy

84A Stafford Road

Whereas Tyseley provided much of the motive power for the local services in the Birmingham area, Wolverhampton Stafford Road supplied locomotives for the main line services. This shed was situated a mile or so north of Wolverhampton Low Level station and stood adjacent to both the locomotive works and Dunstall Park station.

The sheds and coaling facilities were spread over quite a large area. The GWR had provided a broad gauge shed on this site as early as 1854; this was rebuilt in 1874 and again just after the turn of the century, leaving a layout that comprised of three roundhouses and various straight sheds. The turntable and coaling plant were some distance away, in the lower shed yard. By the late 1930s two of the roundhouses had fallen into disuse, and over the ensuing years became semi-derelict. Between the wars the shed had a good selection of GW 4-6-0 types, firstly 'Stars' and 'Saints' then followed in the 1930s and 1940s by the newer 'Castles' and 'Kings'. By the mid-1950s over half of the allocation comprised of these 4-6-0 passenger types. The last 'Star', No 4061 *Glastonbury Abbey*, was withdrawn from

Stafford Road in 1957. During this period the shed itself always had a run-down appearance. This was not, however, reflected by either locomotives or crews, as some of the finest work on the cut-off route was being performed at this time by Stafford Road men.

The introduction in 1960 of one-hour services to London saw Stafford Road become the hub of locomotive activity on the line, with no fewer than 27 of the 'King' class engines being allocated to these services, 11 of them at Stafford Road. This, however, was not to last for too long as the 'Kings' were withdrawn in September 1962 and the shed complex itself, never having been used for diesels, closed just a year later in September 1963.

Allocation

'5700' class	0-6-0PT	3615, 3664, 3756, 3778, 3792, 8726, 8796, 8798
'6400' class	0-6-0PT	6418, 6422
'9400' class	0-6-0PT	8411, 8425, 8426, 8461, 9428, 9435, 9496
'5101' class	2-6-2T	5151, 5187
'Hall' class	4-6-0	4901 *Adderley Hall*; 5900 *Hinderton Hall*; 5926 *Grotrian Hall*; 6926 *Holkham Hall*
'Castle' class	4-6-0	4078 *Pembroke Castle*; 5019 *Treago Castle*; 5022 *Wigmore Castle*; 5026 *Criccieth Castle*; 5031 *Totnes Castle*; 5045 *Earl of Dudley*; 5046 *Earl Cawdor*; 5047 *Earl of Dartmouth*; 5063 *Earl Baldwin*; 5070 *Sir Daniel Gooch*; 5072 *Hurricane*; 5088 *Llanthony Abbey*; 5089 *Westminster Abbey*; 7015 *Kingswear Castle*; 7026 *Tenby Castle*
'King' class	4-6-0	6001 *King Edward VII*; 6005 *King George II*; 6006 *King George I*; 6007 *King William III*; 6008 *King James II*; 6011 *King James I*; 6014 *King Henry VII*; 6017 *King Edward IV*; 6020 *King Henry IV*; 6022 *King Edward III*

Total: 48

84B Oxley

With the growth of rail traffic in the Wolverhampton area, it soon became apparent that the cramped engine shed at Stafford Road needed some relief. This was provided by the GWR in the form of a brand-new engine shed at Oxley. Opened in July 1907, it was situated approximately ¼-mile north of Stafford Road on the Shrewsbury line.

The main shed building measured 450ft × 180ft, and housed within its structure were two turntables each with 28 bays. The shed itself was situated alongside Oxley Sidings and was provided with a large allocation of goods and mixed traffic engines. Like other ex-Great Western depots in the area, Oxley passed into the hands of the LMR in 1963 and was coded 2B. When Stafford Road was closed, many of its engines found their way here and for some time the allocation included eight 'Castles'. Although many ex-LMS types were subsequently allocated to Oxley, it still retained a good number of ex-GWR types in its allocation. Oxley was one of the last depots to remain open to steam in the area, finally closing in March 1967.

Allocation

Class	Wheel	Numbers
'5700' class	0-6-0PT	3698, 7759, 9739, 9752, 9768
'9400' class	0-6-0PT	8428, 8462, 9408
'2800' class	2-8-0	2841, 2850, 2859, 3802, 3813, 3820, 3829, 3861, 3865
'4300' class	2-6-0	6353, 7339, 7341
'5600' class	0-6-2T	6640, 6645
'7200' class	2-8-2T	7217, 7247
'Grange' class	4-6-0	6806 *Blackwell Grange*; 6817 *Gwenddwr Grange*; 6839 *Hewell Grange*; 6857 *Tudor Grange*; 6862 *Derwent Grange*
'Hall' class	4-6-0	4951 *Pendeford Hall*; 4957 *Postlip Hall*; 4963 *Rignall Hall*; 4966 *Shakenhurst Hall*; 4984 *Albrighton Hall*; 4997 *Elton Hall*; 5916 *Trinity Hall*; 5919 *Worsley Hall*; 5944 *Ickenham Hall*; 5965 *Woollas Hall*; 5985 *Mostyn Hall*; 5991 *Gresham Hall*; 5995 *Wick Hall*; 6907 *Davenham Hall*; 6925 *Hackness Hall*; 6934 *Beachamwell Hall*.
'Modified Hall' class	4-6-0	6975 *Capesthorne Hall*; 6980 *Llanrumney Hall*; 7915 *Mere Hall*

Total: 48

84C Banbury

The Great Western Railway opened its new engine shed at Banbury on 29 September 1908. It replaced a small single road shed provided by the same company during 1889, to service engines from the newly opened branch to Kingham. Motive power at this time was being supplied by either Oxford or Leamington.

The opening of the Great Central connection at Banbury Junction in 1900 saw the requirement for better locomotive servicing facilities at Banbury. These were provided by the GWR in the form of a brand-new shed, situated approximately 20 chains south of Banbury station on land bordered by the nearby River Cherwell. The new shed was a four-road brick-built structure measuring 67ft × 210ft. A 55ft turntable stood alongside the rear of the shed adjacent to the nearby River Cherwell. In the shed yard stood a brick-built double-sided coaling stage over which was situated a 45,000gal water tank.

The initial allocation of about 25 locomotives was gradually increased over the years. In 1930, for instance, it

Below:
This general view of Banbury depot yard was taken in 1964 nearly a year after the shed had passed into the control of London Midland Region. Ex-GWR classes are still at this time in the majority; left to right are 2-8-0 No 3845, 'Hall' No 6923 *Croxteth Hall* and 'Modified Hall' No 7912 *Little Linford Hall*. T. Longstaffe

had risen to 49 and by the start of World War 2 to 58. A vast increase in wartime traffic saw the allocation rise during 1943 to nearly 80 locomotives, some of which were examples of LMS and LNER classes on loan. Plans for extending the shed buildings in 1943 did not materialise, with only an extra four roads of tracks being laid. During 1944 the locomotive yard was relaid with extra sidings which together with the provision of a new lifting shop, an extended coaling plant and two new ash shelters, greatly increased the capacity of the shed.

By 1959 the locomotive allocation had dropped back to 52. Always essentially a goods shed, the locomotive stock was interestingly supplemented over the winter of 1959/60 with the allocation for the first time of

three 'Castle' class 4-6-0s, Nos 4078, 5057 and 7011, the last aptly named *Banbury Castle*. These were used for working Banbury-Paddington and Paddington-Wolverhampton semi-fast duties, the latter service via Oxford.

Banbury, as with the other '84' division sheds, passed into the hands of the LMR during September 1963; the result was not only a change of shed code to 2D, but also the allocation of large numbers of ex-LMS and BR Standard types, including a number of 'Britannia' class 4-6-2s. During the last few years of its existence, Banbury shed was to become the graveyard for many withdrawn steam locomotives, when they were cut up on site by the nearby firm of James Friswell. The shed was closed completely during October 1966.

Allocation

Class	Wheel	Numbers
'5700' class	0-6-0PT	3646, 7761
'9400' class	0-6-0PT	8452, 9449
'5400' class	0-6-0PT	5407, 5420, 6429
'2251' class	0-6-0	2256, 2297
'2800' class	2-8-0	2890, 3816, 3856
'4300' class	2-6-0	6311, 6387, 7305, 7308, 7315
'5101' class	2-6-2T	4149, 5152, 5170
'WD' class	2-8-0	90148, 90313, 90585
Standard '9F'	2-10-0	92212, 92226, 92227, 92228, 92232, 92233, 92234, 92250
'Hall' class	4-6-0	4942 *Maindy Hall*, 4964 *Rodwell Hall*, 4990 *Clifton Hall*, 5921 *Bingley Hall*, 5930 *Hannington Hall*, 5947 *Saint Benets Hall*, 5989 *Cransley Hall*, 6906 *Chicheley Hall*, 6929 *Whorlton Hall*, 6949 *Haberfield Hall*,
'Modified Hall' class	4-6-0	6976 *Graythwaite Hall*, 6979 *Helperly Hall*

Total: 43

Banbury shed on 27 June 1965 has, from left to right, 'Modified Hall' No 7920 *Coney Hall*, Stanier '8F' No 48354 and Standard '9F' No 92128. By this date ex-GW types were in the minority here. Mike Soden

For quite a while after their withdrawal many of the 'King' class were stored prior to being broken up. In October 1963 No 6027 *King Richard I* stands in Banbury shed yard, its valve gear dismantled, but still almost intact nearly a year after its official withdrawal. Mike Soden

84D Leamington

The engine shed at Leamington was opened during September 1906 and replaced an earlier shed built in 1852 and destroyed by fire, which stood near the north end of Leamington station. This new shed was situated to the south of the station and stood between the GW main line and the LNWR line from Leamington to Rugby. A four-road brick-built straight shed, measuring 180ft × 66ft, it had an allocation of some 30 locomotives, mainly for intermediate services on the lines to both Moor Street and Snow Hill and also services to and from Stratford-upon-Avon via Hatton.

During the 1950s the bulk of the allocation comprised of ex-GW 2-6-2Ts. In 1958 the nearby ex-LNWR shed at Warwick Milverton Road was closed, which resulted in several ex-LMS locomotives being allocated to Leamington. Dieselisation of the local services in the late 1950s saw the allocation drop to just 20 steam engines. In July 1959, DMU servicing facilities were opened at the nearby carriage sidings.

Regional boundary changes during September 1963 saw the shed pass into London Midland Region control, being recoded 2L, with the resulting influx of ex-LMS and Standard types. However, when the shed was closed on 13 June 1965, three ex-GWR '5600' class 0-6-2Ts Nos 6644, 6671, 6697 were in its final allocation.

Allocation

'5700' class	0-6-0PT	3619, 3624, 3631, 7702
'5101' class	2-6-2T	4112, 4118, 4162, 4171, 5101, 5184
'5600' class	0-6-2T	6657, 6697
'8100' class	2-6-2T	8100, 8109
Ivatt '2MT'	2-6-2T	41228
Staner '4MT'	2-6-4T	42566
'WD' class	2-8-0	90483

Total: 17

84E Tyseley

Tyseley engine shed was opened in June 1908, and was a direct replacement for the old GW sheds at Bordesley, which had served the company since 1855. The new shed at Tyseley was a splendid affair, the large brick shell measured some 220ft×360ft and housed within its walls two 65ft turntables each with 28 bays. Alongside stood a 12-road lifting and repair shop. The large coaling plant and water tank stood adjacent to the shed in the extensive locomotive yard.

The depot provided much of the motive power for the South Birmingham suburban services, and it also had a large allocation of goods and shunting engines, which operated from the many yards in the area. Up until the mid-1950s Tyseley had an allocation of around 100 engines. However, with the introduction of diesel multiple-units on to many of the suburban services during 1957, this total dropped to around 70. The large carriage sidings that stood adjacent to the shed were gradually given over to the accommodation of DMUs. Servicing for these was provided with the conversion of part of the lifting shop into a diesel servicing depot, which opened on 1 July 1958.

By June 1962 Tyseley was the home for 55 steam locomotives and 58 diesel sets. Regional boundary changes in 1963 saw the shed pass into the hands of the London Midland Region, being coded 2A. Right up until 1965 the shed retained a good-sized allocation of ex-GWR classes, and when the depot was finally closed to steam in November 1966 it still housed the last three standard gauge GW locomotives in service; 0-6-0PTs Nos 4646, 4696 and 9774, which ensured that the shed retained its GW tradition to the end.

Allocation

Class	Wheel	Numbers
'5700' class	0-6-0PT	3625, 3657, 3660, 3673, 3693, 4648, 5745, 7763, 8700, 9614, 9635, 9680, 9682, 9724, 9727, 9733, 9753, 9798
'9400' class	0-6-0PT	8415, 8468, 9432
'2251' class	0-6-0	2211, 2257, 2267
'2800' class	2-8-0	2849, 2886
'4300' class	2-6-0	5369, 6399, 7317
'5101' class	2-6-2T	4111, 4126, 4155, 4170, 4172, 5163, 5192
'5600' class	0-6-2T	5658, 6631, 6668
'6100' class	2-6-2T	6105, 6116, 6139, 6160
'7400' class	0-6-0PT	7424
'8100' class	2-6-2T	8108
'Hall' class	4-6-0	4974 *Talgarth Hall*; 4982 *Acton Hall*; 5912 *Queens Hall*; 5927 *Guild Hall*
'Modified Hall' class	4-6-0	6971 *Athelhampton Hall*; 7908 *Henshall Hall*; 7912 *Little Linford Hall*; 7918 *Rhose Wood Hall*
'Manor' class	4-6-0	7824 *Iford Manor*
'Grange' class	4-6-0	6853 *Morehampton Grange*; 6861 *Crynant Grange*; 6866 *Morfa Grange*
BR Standard		
Class 4	4-6-0	75005, 75006, 75024

Total: 60

Left:
This general view of Tyseley shed yard was taken on 22 November 1964, and shows from left to right, 'Manor' class 4-6-0 No 7805 Broome Manor, Standard '9F' 2-10-0 No 92237 and an unidentified '4100' 2-6-2T. The carriage and DMU sidings can be seen to the left.
M. Mensing

Above:
The interior of Tyseley roundhouse on 3 July 1962 contains, from left to right, 0-6-0 pannier tanks Nos 9798 and 7426 together with 2-6-2T No 4155 and 0-6-2T No 6631. Richard McAvoy

Wolverhampton Works

As already mentioned, adjacent to Stafford Road shed stood the Wolverhampton Works of the GWR. Built in 1849 by the Shrewsbury & Birmingham Railway Co as a locomotive depot and repair shops, they were taken over and enlarged by the Great Western Railway in 1854 when the two companies amalgamated. Locomotive building commenced here during 1859 and gradually the site was extended by the provision of a new erecting shop. During these early days the works were under the supervision of the Armstrongs, firstly Joseph, and after his transfer to Swindon to succeed Gooch in 1863, his brother George. When he retired in

1897 the works were placed under the overall control of Swindon. Locomotive building ceased at Wolverhampton in 1908, with a grand total of some 794 locomotives being constructed.

In 1929 the GWR decided to completely rebuild the works, and when the work was finished during 1932 the result was a building of some 450ft long by 196ft wide, housing within its walls new erecting, machine and wheel shops. This now gave the Great

Western a modern overflow for Swindon. The new works now allowed the heaviest locomotives to be repaired. In 1959 some 310 locomotives and 183 boilers passed through the works. Locomotive repairs continued until 11 February 1964, by which time the works were under the control of the London Midland Region. Being surplus to requirements, they closed shortly afterwards. The last engine to be outshopped was Churchward 2-8-0 No 2859.

Locomotives under repair in Wolverhampton Works Sunday 1 November 1959

Class	Type	Numbers
'5700' class	0-6-0PT	3650, 3665, 4614, 4644, 4696, 7760, 8797, 9656, 9774
'7400' class	0-6-0PT	7436
'9400' class	0-6-0PT	8403
'1400' class	0-4-2T	1440
'5400' class	0-6-0PT	5414
'2551' class	0-6-0	3205
'4500' class	2-6-2T	4565
'6100' class	2-6-2T	6145
'4300' class	2-6-0	7308, 7324
'2800' class	2-8-0	2849, 3814
'5600' class	0-6-2T	5635, 5658, 5659, 5672, 6602, 6656, 6691
'Hall' class	4-6-0	4994 *Downton Hall*
'Castle' class	4-6-0	5018 *St Mawes Castle*
Standard '2MT'	2-6-2T	82005
Ivatt '2MT'	2-6-0	46523

Total: 31

6
The Route Today

Today it is still possible to travel via the cut-off route from Paddington to a new station at Birmingham Snow Hill, although to complete the journey one has to change trains at Banbury or Leamington. Unfortunately Wolverhampton cannot now be reached via the old Great Western route, as much of that line has now been lifted.

From Banbury southwards the cut-off route is now back under the control of the Western Region, with services being operated by Network SouthEast. Today Banbury is the northern terminus for 'Chiltern line' services to and from Marylebone. These are still operated by the same DMUs that were introduced on to the line in 1962. Currently there are 11 trains in each direction between Banbury and Marylebone with one locomotive-hauled train each weekday between Banbury and Paddington. Departing at 07.15, it returns in the evening at 17.53, calling at most stations en route. This is currently diagrammed for Class 50 haulage. Apart from this one working no regular passenger services now use the section between Old Oak Junction and Northolt other than in an emergency. A feature of the route between here and Princes Risborough is the retention in many places of semaphore signalling, and at the time of writing

boxes are still open at Greenford, Northolt, West Ruislip, Gerrards Cross, High Wycombe and Princes Risborough. A recent proposal is for a new power box to be installed at High Wycombe which will control the route from Northolt right through to Aynho.

Other than West Wycombe, which was closed in 1958, all stations south of Princes Risborough are still open. Track rationalisation has seen the removal of many of the yards and sidings, together with the through running lines at Beaconsfield, Gerrards Cross and Denham.

Few freight services nowadays

traverse the south end of the route. Domestic coal is supplied to Neasden and Aylesbury via the 09.15 Speedlink service from Didcot. This travels via Acton to Neasden and then via Northolt Junction to Aylesbury, arriving at 13.18. Thame oil terminal currently has a daily delivery from Thames Haven; this again runs via Acton.

Freight services on the section northwards from Aynho Junction comprise mainly coal and Freightliner services. Didcot power station is currently supplied by 17 daily MGR trains. These enter the route at either Bordesley Junction or the ex-LNWR

Right:
The 1.10pm Paddington-Wolverhampton service passes Royal Oak hauled by No 7030 *Cranbrook Castle* on 26 August 1962. The siding in the background serves the large Guinness Brewery, whilst the Central Line extension can be seen to the right. M. Pope

Above right:
'Hall' class 4-6-0 No 5912 *Queens Hall* approaches Lapworth on Sunday 5 May 1957 with a special train of boy scouts. Both up and down main lines at this point have just been dug out and relaid, and reballasting can be seen in progress. M. Mensing

Far right:
The unusual sight of Fowler 2-6-4T No 42343 on the 5.10pm service from Birmingham Snow Hill to Knowle & Dorridge, seen here approaching Acocks Green station on 11 April 1961.
M. Mensing

branch from Coventry to Leamington. Harbury cement works is closed for cement production; nowadays it is just a distribution depot, supplied once a week by bulk cement from Weardale (Durham) to Greaves' Sidings via the BR Speedlink service.

The section of the original Wycombe Railway from High Wycombe to Bourne End was closed in 1970, and little evidence of this line now exists at the Wycombe end. At High Wycombe itself the station complex has changed little. Although many of the goods

sidings have been removed, the main line layout through the station is still mostly intact. Semaphore signalling is very much in evidence here, being controlled from the Wycombe South box. The one intermediate station between High Wycombe and Princes

Risborough, Saunderton is now an unstaffed halt. At Princes Risborough the down side platforms have been closed and removed; all trains now use the up platform, trackwork and signalling being modified to allow two-way working.

The large signalbox at Risborough North is still open and currently controls the cut-off route as far as Aynho Junction. The branch to Aylesbury is now served by trains to and from Marylebone, giving a frequency of 11 services daily in each direction. The other two branches here are still partially open for freight only; the

Watlington branch as far as Chinnor cement works, and the Oxford branch to an oil terminal at Thame. From Princes Risborough to Aynho Junction the track has now been singled, but a passing point is still retained at Bicester North. At Ashendon it is now difficult to imagine the large flying junction that was once situated here; practically all trace of it is now gone, only the grass embankment of the flyover is still visible.

Good news during 1987 was the opening on 3 October by Network SouthEast of a new station, Haddenham & Thame Parkway, built to serve the nearby rapidly expanding town of Thame. This, together with Bicester North, are now the only two stations on the cut-off section. At Bicester North the down platform is now used for two-way working; although the up platform is retained, it is little used. Bicester also had cause to celebrate in 1987 with the experimental reopening of a service to Oxford. The old LNWR station at Bicester London Road has been revamped and renamed Bicester Town. Moving along the line, the limestone quarry at Ardley is now closed and the sidings lifted. The two-way junction at Aynho remains almost unchanged with both up and down lines still in situ, as is the junction signalbox. Approaching King's Sutton, part of the brick viaduct can still be seen on the closed branch to Kingham. King's Sutton station is now an unstaffed halt; the fine stone station buildings have long been removed.

Banbury today is a pale shadow of its former self. The site of the large engine shed, to the south of the station, is now but an overgrown wasteland. Banbury station itself remains almost unaltered, the empty bay platforms a reminder of the once busy branch services to Woodford. It is probably the reduction of goods traffic that has brought the most change to Banbury, for the once large hump yard is now reduced to just a few sidings. At the time of writing the two manual signalboxes at Banbury station North and South are still open. The remains of the Oxford Ironstone Railway are now almost completely obliterated by the new housing developments and industrial sites which have spread to the northwest of Banbury.

Express passenger services on this section are now provided by InterCity cross-country trains running via the Oxford line. Intermediate services northward now run between Banbury and the new station at Snow Hill Although there are now no longer any stations open between Banbury and Leamington, at the time of writing two manual signalboxes still survive. The first is situated at Fenny Compton and controls the remains of the Stratford-upon-Avon & Midland Junction branch that today terminates at Kineton ordnance depot. The second box still in use is at Greaves' Sidings south of Harbury, which controls the sidings to the adjacent cement works.

Leamington station is another on the line that is relatively unchanged;

its bays and through running lines being retained. A new experimental electronic signalbox recently opened here has replaced the 121-lever frame North box. North of Leamington the route into Birmingham is now under the control of Saltley power box, with all intermediate boxes removed. The site of the ex-LNWR station at Leamington Avenue which closed in 1966 is nowadays covered by a small industrial estate, as is the engine shed site to the south of the station. Main line services currently leave the ex-GW route here and run via the ex-LNWR branch to Coventry. At Hatton the South Junction remains for the Leamington-Stratford service, but the line from here to Bearley has now been singled once again. A feature in the 1988 timetable is a new HST Pullman service running between Paddington, Oxford and Stratford-upon-Avon.

Surprisingly all of the stations between Hatton and Birmingham are still in use although some are now

unstaffed halts. The four-track layout between Lapworth and Tyseley has now been reduced to just two. Tyseley is now the major servicing point for both main line diesels and DMUs in the Birmingham area. What is left of the old steam depot now forms part of Birmingham Railway Museum; here various examples of GW motive power can be seen operating on open days.

Under the auspices of the West Midlands PTE, a new station has once again been opened at Snow Hill, the tracks being reinstated through the tunnel once again. Prior to its opening on 2 October, the general public were invited to walk through the refurbished tunnel, and astonishingly over 14,000 took up the option. At the same time a new through station was opened at Moor Street. The old terminus was closed from 5 October 1987. It is however being retained as a potential steam museum. All North Warwicks line and Banbury-Birmingham DMU services now use

the new station at Snow Hill. A more enlightened attitude to promoting services has seen passenger usage over the whole of the remaining route increase enormously during the last few years. Between Snow Hill and Wolverhampton the through railway has completely gone. Several small parts of the route still exist, notably around the Wednesbury area serving various yards and sidings. Wolverhampton Low Level station still survives however, having been used for many years as a parcels depot. It is to be hoped that it will soon see a new lease of life as a heritage museum.

To conclude on a happy note, steam traction is once again in evidence over much of the route. In recent years a feature of Sunday workings has been the running of 'Luncheon Specials' between Marylebone and Stratford-upon-Avon with steam haulage throughout. Steam specials from Didcot Railway Centre to Stratford-upon-Avon and Tyseley have been operated successfully for quite a number of years now. Recently the North Warwicks line has also been used for steam excursions between Moor Street and Stratford, using preserved engines from Tyseley.

Perhaps we should be thankful that not only can we still travel over the last main line to be built in the country, but that we can still on occasions do it in style behind steam traction.

Appendices

1 Main Line Passenger Workings Saturday 13 June 1959

Down Services

Train	Destination	Locomotive	Shed	Load
09.00	Pwllheli	6019 *King Henry V*	81A	8
09.10	Birkenhead	6029 *King Edward VIII*	81A	12
10.10*	Aberystwyth	6010 *King Charles I*	81A	12
11.10	Birkenhead	6008 *King James II*	84A	10
2.10	Birkenhead	6005 *King George II*	84A	13
4.10	Birkenhead	6001 *King Edward VII*	84A	12
4.34	Banbury	6929 *Whorlton Hall*	84C	4
6.10	Wolverhampton	6014 *King Henry VII*	84A	12

Up Services

Train	From	Locomotive	Shed	Load
06.30	Birkenhead	6001 *King Edward VII*	84A	12
06.45	Wolverhampton	6008 *King James II*	84A	15
Exc	Bilston	5072 *Hurricane*	84A	11
Exc	Wolverhampton	5019 *Treago Castle*	84A	9
07.30	Shrewsbury	6005 *King George II*	84A	13
08.55	Birkenhead	6014 *King Henry VII*	84A	11
11.45	Birkenhead	6011 *King James I*	84A	10
11.45*	Aberystwyth	4918 *Dartington Hall*	84A	12

* 'Cambrian Coast Express'
Exc Excursion
81A Old Oak Common
84A Wolverhampton Stafford Road
84C Banbury

The departure time of the two excursions was not known.

2 Stations on the Wolverhampton Direct Route

Station	Opened	Closed	Station	Opened	Closed
Old Oak Lane halt	1.10.06	30. 6.47	Saunderton†	1. 7.01	
North Acton*	5.11.23	30. 6.47	Princes Risborough	1. 8.1854	
North Acton halt	1. 5.04	1. 2.13	Ilmer halt	1. 4.29	7. 1.63
Park Royal	15. 6.03	26. 9.37	Haddenham	1. 7.1863	7. 1.63
Park Royal West halt	20. 6.32	30. 6.47	Haddenham & Thame Parkway	3.10.87	new station
Twyford Abbey	1. 5.04	1. 5.11	Dorton halt	21. 6.37	7. 1.63
Brentham halt*	1. 5.11	30. 6.47	Brill & Ludgershall	1. 7.10	7. 1.63
Perivale halt*	1. 5.04	30. 6.47	Blackthorn	1. 7.10	8. 6.53
Greenford*	1.10.04	17. 6.63	Bicester North	1. 7.10	
Northolt halt*	1. 5.07	21.11.48	Ardley	1. 7.10	7. 1.63
Northolt Junction (South Ruislip)	1. 7.08	LRT/BR	Aynho Park halt	1. 7.10	7. 1.63
			Kings Sutton†	2. 8.1872	
Ruislip Gardens*	9. 7.34	21. 7.58	Banbury (rebuilt 1958)	2.10.1850	
Ruislip & Ickenham (West Ruislip)	2. 4.06		Cropredy	1.10.1852	17. 9.56
			Fenny Compton	1.10.1852	2.11.64
Harefield halt	24. 9.28	30. 9.31	Southam Road & Harbury	1.10.1852	2.11.64
Denham	2. 4.06		Leamington	1.10.1852	
Denham Golf Club†	7. 8.12		Warwick	1.10.1852	
Gerrards Cross	2. 4.06		Hatton	1.10.1852	
Beaconsfield Golf Links halt (Seer Green & Jordans)	1. 1.15		Lapworth (opened as Kingswood)	1.10.1854	
Beaconsfield	2. 4.06		Knowle & Dorridge	1.10.1852	
High Wycombe	1. 8.1854		Widney Manor†	1. 7.1899	
West Wycombe	1. 8.1854	3.11.58	Solihull	1.10.1852	

Station	Opened	Closed	Station	Opened	Closed
Olton	1.11.1869		West Bromwich	14.11.1854	6. 3.72
Acocks Green & South Yardley	1.10.1852		Swan Village	14.11.1854	6. 3.72
Tyseley	1.10.06		Wednesbury Central	14.11.1854	6. 3.72
Small Heath & Sparkbrook	1. 7.1863		Bradley & Moxley	1. 1.1862	1. 1.17
Bordesley†	1. 1.1855		Bilston	14.11.1854	6. 3.72
Snow Hill (Old)	1.10.1852	6. 3.72	Priestfield (GWR/OW&WR)	1. 7.1854	6. 3.72
Snow Hill (New)	5.10.87	new station	Wolverhampton Low Level	14.11.1854	6. 3.72
Hockley	14.11.1854	6. 3.72			
Soho & Winson Green	14.11.1854	6. 3.72			
Handsworth & Smethwick	14.11.1854	6. 3.72			
The Hawthorns halt	25.12.31	27. 4.68			

* Replaced by new stations on LT Central line extension.
† Unstaffed halt

3a Distances
Paddington-Birmingham-Wolverhampton

Location	Distance (miles)	Location	Distance (miles)
PADDINGTON	0.00	Southam Road	81.10
Old Oak Common West box (D)	3.25	Fosse Road box (D)	83.55
Park Royal box	4.80	LEAMINGTON SPA	87.35
Greenford	7.80	Warwick	89.30
Northolt Jcn East box (D)	10.05	Hatton	93.45
South Ruislip	10.25	Hatton North Jcn box	93.90
West Ruislip	12.10	Lapworth	97.65
Denham	14.80	Knowle & Dorridge	100.20
Denham Golf Club	15.65	Widney Manor	102.10
Gerrards Cross	17.45	Solihull	104.60
Seer Green & Jordans	20.15	Olton	105.40
Beaconsfield	21.70	Acocks Green	106.40
HIGH WYCOMBE	26.55	Tyseley	107.35
West Wycombe	28.80	Small Heath	108.45
Saunderton	31.55	Bordesley	109.35
PRINCES RISBOROUGH	34.70	Moor Street	110.15
Ilmer halt	37.40	BIRMINGHAM SNOW HILL	110.65
Haddenham	40.10	Hockley·	111.55
Ashendon Jcn box (a)	44.05	Soho & Winson Green	112.20
Brill halt	47.45	Handsworth	113.20
Blackthorn	50.45	Handsworth Jcn box (U)	113.85
BICESTER NORTH	53.40	West Bromwich	115.35
Ardley halt	57.20	Swan Village	116.45
Aynho Park	61.50	Wednesbury Central	118.15
Aynho Jcn box	62.40	Bilston Central	120.40
Kings Sutton	63.95	Priestfield	121.50
BANBURY	67.50	WOLVERHAMPTON LOW LEVEL	123.05
Banbury Jcn box (D)	68.65		
Cropredy	71.10		
Claydon Crossing box (D)	73.60	(U) Up	
Fenny Compton	76.25	(D) Down side of line	
Knightcote box (D)	78.35	(a) Between down and up lines	

3b Distances
Birmingham - Stratford-upon-Avon

Location	Distance (miles)	Location	Distance (miles)
Birmingham (Snow Hill)	0.00	Wootton Wawen platform	18.75
Birmingham (Moor Street)*	0.50	Bearley North Jcn box	20.75
Tyseley	3.30	Hatton North Jcn box†	16.75
Hall Green	4.80	Hatton West Jcn box†	17.15
Yardley Wood	6.05	Claverdon†	18.40
Shirley	7.30	Bearley†	21.75
Whitlocks End halt	8.20	Bearley West Jnc box	21.30
Grimes Hill & Wythall	9.20	Wilmcote	22.35
Earlswood Lakes	10.20	Stratford-upon-Avon	25.00
The Lakes halt	11.20		
Wood End	12.15		
Danzey for Tanworth	14.00	* Terminus	
Henley-in-Arden	16.95	† Down mileage via Stratford	

4 Tunnels

Tunnel	No of lines	Length
White House	2	348yd
Saunderton (up line)	1	84yd
Brill	2	193yd
Ardley	2	1,147yd
Harbury	2	73yd
Snow Hill	2	596yd
Hockley No 1	4	132yd
Hockley No 2	5	160yd
Swan Village	2	412yd
Wolverhampton (down)	1	377yd
Wolverhampton (up)	1	377yd

5 Water Troughs

Situated between	Lines served	Length
Denham and West Ruislip	both main	560yd
Aynho and Kings Sutton	both main	560yd
Hatton and Rowington Jcn	both main	560yd

Fenny Compton is the location as No 7922 passes with a Shrewsbury-Didcot stores working on 11 June 1965.
J. R. P. Hunt

Sources & Acknowledgements

Information on the history and workings of the line has been found in the following locations:
Public Record Office, Kew
The Local History Library, Oxford
The Oxfordshire County Records Office
BTHR Porchester Road, London
The Great Western Society Small Relics Museum, Didcot

Other sources have been:
Trains Illustrated
Railway World
Railway Magazine
Locomotive Review
Bradshaw's Guides
Journal of Transport History
and many BR Timetables and Working Instructions.

I would like to thank the following persons who have contributed photographs and information: J. Hubbard, W. Turner, B. Higgins, J. D. Edwards, R. McAvoy, Dr G. Smith, S. Creer, B. Morrison, C. R. L. Coles, M. Soden, M. Mensing, A. Doyle, D. Tuck, S. Dart and the Ian Allan Library.

Special thanks to my wife Carol for deciphering my original writing and typing the manuscript, also to Peter Webber, Brian Matthews and Tim Davey-Winter for their comments on the manuscript and to Sharon FitzPatrick-Titterton for word processing the final draft, and last but not least Dave Kozlow for the diagrams.

Bibliography

History of the Great Western Railway Vols 1, 2, 3 E. T. McDermot
The Final Link R. Pigram/ D. Edwards
Clinker's Register of GW Halts and Platforms C. Clinker
Salute to Snow Hill D. Harrison
The Great Great Western W. J. Scott
The Armstrongs of the Great Western H. Holcroft
The GW and GC Joint Railway S. Jenkins
Titled Trains of Great Britain C. J. Allen
Locomotives of the GWR Parts 1-13 RCTS
Regional History of the Railways of Britain (Chiltern and Cotswolds) R. Davies
Regional History of the Railways of Britain (West Midlands) R. Christiansen

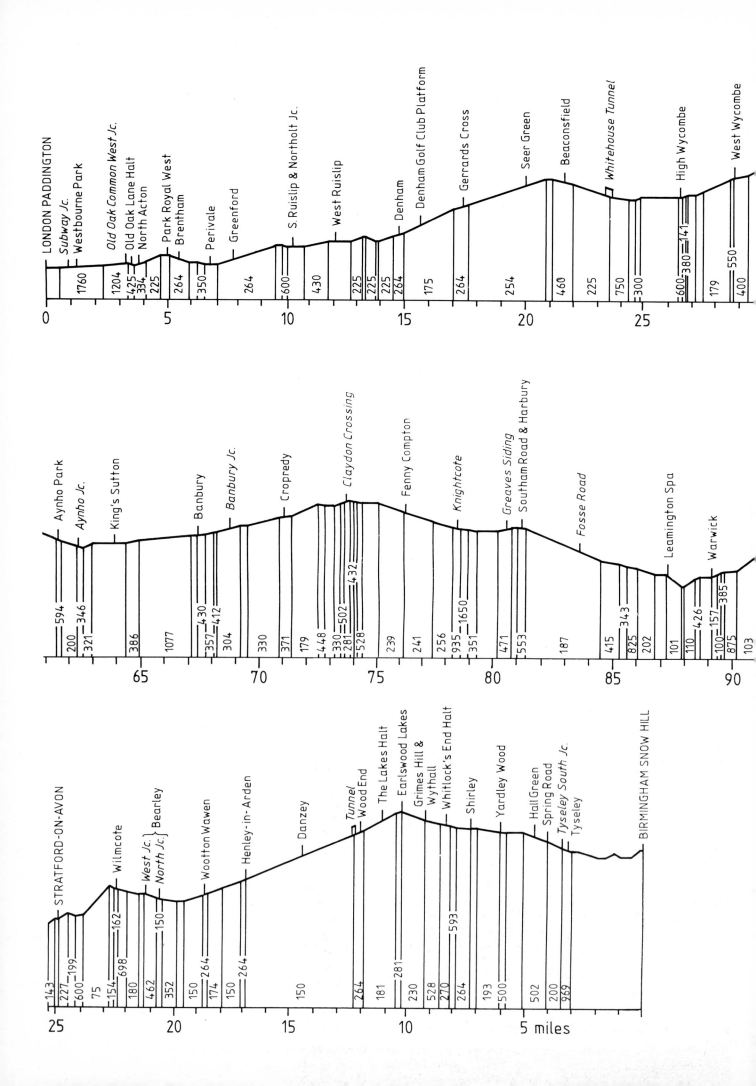